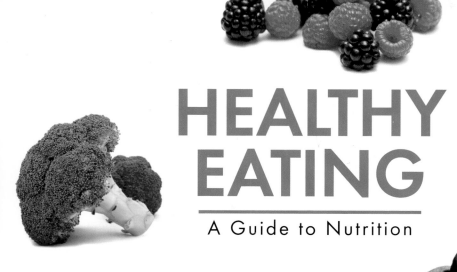

HEALTHY EATING

A Guide to Nutrition

Nutrition and Disease Prevention

HEALTHY EATING: A GUIDE TO NUTRITION

HEALTHY EATING

A Guide to Nutrition

Nutrition and Disease Prevention

Toney Allman

CHELSEA HOUSE
PUBLISHERS

An imprint of Infobase Publishing

Chelsea House
An imprint of Infobase Publishing
132 West 31st Street
New York, NY 10001

Library of Congress Cataloging-in-Publication Data
Allman, Toney.
    Nutrition and disease prevention / Toney Allman.
        p. cm. — (Healthy eating: a guide to nutrition)
    Includes bibliographical references and index.
    ISBN 978-1-60413-777-4 (hardcover)
    1. Nutrition. 2. Medicine, Preventive. I. Title. II. Series.
    QP141.A635 2010
    612.3—dc22   2009041337

Chelsea House books are available at special discounts when purchased in bulk quantities for businesses, associations, institutions, or sales promotions. Please call our Special Sales Department in New York at (212) 967-8800 or (800) 322-8755.

You can find Chelsea House on the World Wide Web
at http://www.chelseahouse.com

Text design and composition by Annie O'Donnell
Cover design by Alicia Post
Cover printed by Bang Printing, Brainerd, Minn.
Book printed and bound by Bang Printing, Brainerd, Minn.
Date printed: July 2010
Printed in the United States of America

10 9 8 7 6 5 4 3 2 1

This book is printed on acid-free paper.

All links and Web addresses were checked and verified to be correct at the time of publication. Because of the dynamic nature of the Web, some addresses and links may have changed since publication and may no longer be valid.

CONTENTS

INTRODUCTION

A hundred years ago, people received nutritional guidance from mothers and grandmothers: Eat your carrots because they're good for your eyes; don't eat too many potatoes because they'll make you fat; be sure to get plenty of roughage so you can more easily move your bowels. Today, everyone seems to offer more advice: Take a vitamin supplement to optimize your health; don't eat fish with cabbage because you won't be able to digest them together; you can't stay healthy on a vegetarian diet. Nutrition is one of those topics about which all people seem to think they know something, or at least have an opinion. Whether it is the clerk in your local health food store recommending that you buy supplements or the woman behind you in line at the grocery store raving about the latest low-carbohydrate diet, everyone is ready to offer you nutritional advice. How do you know what to believe or, more importantly, what to do?

The purpose of these books is to help you answer these questions. Even if you don't love learning about science, at the very least you probably enjoy certain foods and want to stay healthy—

or become healthier. In response to this, these books are designed to make the science you *need* to understand as palatable as the foods you love. Once you understand the basics, you can apply this simple health knowledge to your everyday decisions about nutrition and health. The **Healthy Eating** set includes one book with all of the basic nutrition information you need to choose a healthy diet, as well as five others that cover topics of special concern to many: weight management, exercise, disease prevention, food safety, and eating disorders.

Our goal is not to tell you to stop eating potato chips and candy bars, give up fast food, or always eat your vegetables. Instead, it is to provide you with the information you need to make informed choices about your diet. We hope you will recognize that potato chips and candy are not poison, but they should only be eaten as occasional treats. We hope you will decide for yourself that fast food is something you can indulge in every now and then, but is not a good choice every day. We encourage you to recognize that although you should eat your vegetables, not everyone always does, so you should do your best to try new vegetables and fruits and eat them as often as possible.

These books take the science of nutrition out of the classroom and allow you to apply this information to the choices you make about foods, exercise, dietary supplements, and other lifestyle decisions that are important to your health. This knowledge should help you choose a healthy diet while allowing you to enjoy the diversity of flavors, textures, and tastes that food provides, while also encouraging you to explore the meanings food holds in our society. When you eat a healthy diet, you will feel good in the short term and enjoy health benefits in the long term. We can't personally evaluate each meal you consume, but we believe these books will give you the tools to make your own nutritious choices.

Lori A. Smolin, Ph.D., and
Mary B. Grosvenor, M.S., R.D.

1

NOURISHING
THE BODY

In the complex, elegant system called the human body, the **nutrients** that are ingested and absorbed are essential for the growth, maintenance, repair, and replacement of the trillions of cells of the organs and tissues that do the body's work. These nutrients are the substances in the foods and beverages we ingest. Nutrition is the sum total of the interaction between the foods we eat—our diets—and the ways in which our bodies process, use, and are nourished by the nutrients in those foods. Although human bodies are incredibly adaptable and may maintain themselves for a long time when nutrition is inadequate or improper, optimum health is dependent on optimum nutrition. When proper amounts of nutrients are lacking or out of balance, or when nutrients are not adequately processed, dysfunction, ill health, and disease are inevitable.

NUTRIENTS FOR LIFE

Scientists and researchers are still learning to define optimal nutrition and understand how nutrients affect health and disease. So far, more than 40 nutrients have been identified as substances that are essential to life. They are grouped into six categories or classes. These classes are carbohydrates, proteins, fats, vitamins, minerals, and water. Carbohydrates, fats, proteins, some minerals, and water are considered to be **macronutrients**, because the body needs them in large quantities. Vitamins and most minerals (often called trace minerals) are needed in relatively small amounts and are referred to as **micronutrients**. They are essential because they enable the body to use its macronutrients. No single food contains all essential nutrients, but most foods are a source of one or more in varying degrees. People must ingest a variety of foods in order to nourish their bodies.

ENERGY AND FUEL

One of the most important functions of nutrients is to provide the fuel that powers the body's functions. **Glucose** is the sugar from carbohydrates that provides the major source of fuel for the body, its organs, and its cells, but fats are another important source. When necessary, proteins can also be used as fuel. These macronutrients provide the body with 100% of its energy. Energy is measured in **calories**. Some foods, such as cheeseburgers, are calorie dense, while others, such as celery, provide few calories. How much food is required to provide enough energy depends on the kinds of foods a person eats, as well as a person's activity level, age, and size. In other words, how much energy is used up and how quickly it is used depends on individual factors and is never standard for all people at all times in their lives.

Because of the energy supplied by these macronutrients, muscles move, lungs breathe, and hearts beat. Bodies use the energy to maintain the correct temperature. Cells build the proteins that do the work in the body. With too few calories, cell activity and organ function falter. A complete lack of energy (meaning zero calories consumed) would lead to cell death and organ failure from starvation within about 8 to 12 weeks. If too many calories are taken in, the body stores the excess as fat, in case extra energy is needed in the future. Every healthy person needs to have some fat stores for emergencies, but an excess amount leads to unhealthy body weight and stress on organs, which also can lead to disease.

ESSENTIAL PROTEIN

When bodies get adequate calories from carbohydrates and fats, they do not use proteins for energy. Instead, protein is used to maintain organs and tissues, for growth, and to build body structures. Living organisms, including human bodies, are basically made of protein. Protein is the primary component of most cells in the body. Because cells are constantly breaking down and dying, they must be continually replaced.

Protein is made of strings of chemical units called **amino acids**. The body's cells can make some of the 20 amino acids that form proteins, but they cannot make 9 of them. These 9 are called essential amino acids because they must be ingested for cells to function. (Only infants need all nine of the essential amino acids; children and adults require eight.) Without the essential amino acids from ingested protein, cells cannot make their own proteins or do work. They cannot build and repair body structures or make the **hormones** and **enzymes** that control the body's chemical reactions. Many hormones and all enzymes are made of protein. Hormones are chemical substances that are the information carriers for cells. They provide signals about what different body parts are supposed to do. Enzymes make the chemical reactions of **metabolism** progress efficiently. They are like the assembly-line workers in the complex factory of each cell.

The body needs access to all of the essential amino acids— complete proteins—at the same time and in the right balance. If no protein is ingested, the body will break down its own body tissues to get the protein it needs. If even one amino acid is missing, severe ill health and death result. If too much of just one amino acid is ingested compared with the others, the body also suffers. The imbalance is toxic, preventing the body from using the other amino acids correctly.

FATTY ACIDS, VITAMINS, AND MINERALS

Fats not only supply calories and energy, but also provide the body with essential substances that it cannot make on its own. These are the essential **fatty acids** required for developing the brain and nervous system, making hormones, maintaining cell membranes,

PROTEINS FROM PLANTS

Although animal food is an easy and complete source of protein, vegetarians and vegans can get proteins from other sources without much difficulty. Vegetarians may eat dairy products and eggs, which provide all the essential amino acids. Vegans need to get their proteins from plant foods. Plants are a protein source, but most plants do not provide all eight essential amino acids. Beans, for example, are high in the amino acid lysine but low in the sulfur-containing amino acids methionine and cysteine. Rice and other whole grains, on the other hand, are low in lysine but rich in the sulfur-containing amino acids. These two food types together, therefore, are complementary proteins. Eaten together, they supply all the essential amino acids needed by people. Legumes, grains, seeds, and nuts can be combined in varying proportions to create complete protein meals. Examples include cornbread and pinto beans, hummus (chickpeas and sesame seeds), and a peanut butter sandwich on whole wheat bread. The only plant foods known to be nearly complete proteins on their own are soybeans, quinoa, buckwheat, and hempseed.

keeping skin healthy, and even maintaining some structures of the eyes. These fatty acids, just like proteins, are also needed so the body can use some vitamins and minerals.

Vitamins and minerals do not provide energy, but they are necessary to keep the body alive and functioning. They are considered to be essential nutrients because, as with essential fatty acids and essential amino acids, they cannot be made by the body. Vitamins are chemical compounds that regulate the body's ability to use food for energy. They also are essential for growth, development, and proper cell functioning. A severe lack of any vitamin leads to disease. Currently, scientists are aware of 13 vitamins essential for health. They are vitamins A, C, D, E, K, and a group of eight B vitamins known by names or numbers. The B vitamins are B1 (thiamine), B2 (riboflavin), B3 (niacin), B5 (pantothenic acid), B6 (pyridoxine), B7 (biotin), B9 (folic acid), and B12 (cobalamin).

The minerals that are macronutrients include calcium, magnesium, salt, and potassium. Bones, muscles, the heart, and the brain depend on these minerals for growth and normal functioning. These minerals also are essential to regulating the functions of nerves and muscles, and keeping the body's fluids in balance. Micronutrient trace minerals, such as copper, iron, zinc, and iodine, are essential parts of hormones and enzymes. Minerals are the same metals that are found in the earth and absorbed by plants, and then by animals that eat the plants. Minerals are toxic in large quantities, but a lack of any of the essential minerals leads to disease.

TURNING FOODS INTO NUTRIENTS

Vitamins and minerals are critical to body metabolism—the chemical reactions that involve building up or breaking down substances in the body. Metabolism is the process by which the body's cells modify nutrient molecules and use them to create energy, or as building blocks for new cells and tissues. Metabolism, for any living organism, is life itself. *Metabolism* comes from a Greek word meaning "change," and that is what cells do with nutrients. They change the chemical substances from foods into molecules that are needed to do the body's work. We do not eat nutrients; we eat foods, which are too chemically complex for cells to use. The foods we eat must be broken down into simpler chemical substances—the nutrients—so that they are available to the cells. Foods go through three steps before nutrients are available to the body's cells. These processes are digestion, absorption, and metabolism.

Digestion begins in the mouth, where teeth and the enzymes in saliva begin breaking down foods. Once in the stomach, food is exposed to gastric juices, and the chemical breakdown turns it into a thick liquid called chyme. Chyme moves to the small intestine. Here, with the help of more chemicals from the pancreas and gallbladder, it is broken down into nutrient components. (Unusable food substances move to the large intestine and are excreted by the body.) The nutrients are now absorbed into the bloodstream through the intestinal walls. Vitamins and minerals can be carried to every cell in the body, via the bloodstream. Amino acids from proteins, glucose from carbohydrates, and fatty acids from fats also are now usable and ready to be metabolized by the cells. The nutrients pass through the cell membranes and into the cells themselves, where more chemical reactions take place.

METABOLISM

Once inside the cell, a molecule of glucose is broken down to release its energy. When nutrient molecules are broken down and energy is released, the process is called **catabolism**. But cells may use energy from nutrients to build more complex molecules, too. For example, a cell membrane may be damaged and need repair. This process is known as **anabolism**. In this case, people use the "bodies" of potatoes, broccoli, and fish, for instance, to maintain and build up their own bodies. The nutrient material in food is

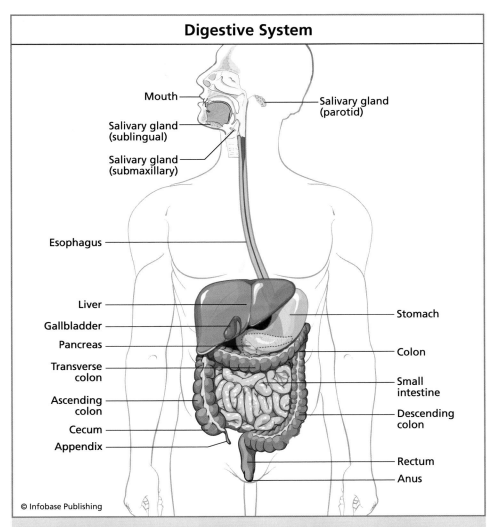

Digestive System

Mouth

Salivary gland (parotid)

Salivary gland (sublingual)

Salivary gland (submaxillary)

Esophagus

Liver

Gallbladder

Pancreas

Transverse colon

Ascending colon

Cecum

Appendix

Stomach

Colon

Small intestine

Descending colon

Rectum

Anus

© Infobase Publishing

FIGURE 1.1 Besides the esophagus, stomach, and small and large intestines, the digestive system includes a tube with an opening at the mouth (for intake) and an opening at the anus (for excretion).

transformed to construct the building blocks of the human body. Scientists say that the nutrients we ingest can be thought of as the metabolic pool used by the cells for construction. Just as carpenters, bricklayers, and roofers use nails, tiles, bricks, mortar, glue, and wood to build a house, cells use the substances from nutrients to construct body parts. The strength of the house depends on the quality of the building materials; the health of the body depends on the quality of the substances in the metabolic pool. To repair a cell membrane, new protein molecules are needed. These will be built through anabolism, using the amino acids in the metabolic pool. The new protein molecules may consist of hundreds or even thousands of amino acids.

Different nutrient molecules may be metabolized in different ways or for different purposes, but all cells' metabolic processes occur in a similar way. Millions of nutrient molecules are absorbed and utilized with every meal. Many end up as part of the body, although some are excreted from the body as unneeded or unusable. Many of these nutrients, especially vitamins, minerals, and proteins, are used to construct or build up enzymes. Enzymes are the chemicals that control the cellular processes of anabolism and catabolism. They also direct how fast a cell's chemical reactions take place. Some vitamins protect the cells from damaging themselves as they metabolize nutrients. Nutrients build new bone, muscle, and blood cells in the body. They fuel the cells that make thinking, moving, and breathing possible. They keep bodies alive by continually building new cells as old ones die. As one example, the Denver Museum of Nature & Science reports that two million red blood cells die and two million are replaced by the blood-manufacturing cells in bone marrow every second. That means an intense, ongoing need for all the proper nutrients.

NUTRITIOUS CHOICES

The body and its cells are dependent upon so many nutrients that it can seem remarkable that anyone is healthy. Yet, humans have survived and thrived for hundreds of thousands of years, long before anyone knew anything about what people should eat every day or what nutrients our bodies require. Humans seem to have evolved to be flexible eaters. People can digest, absorb, and metabolize a variety of plant and animal foods, and our Stone

Age hunter-gatherer ancestors—living more than 10,000 years ago—apparently were able to survive by following their natural food preferences. They may have been ignorant of nutritional science, but the foods they chose nourished their bodies. They ate plants, roots, fruits, berries, nuts, and game animals of all kinds. They had to cope with periods of feasts alternating with periods of famine, so whenever fats were available (which wasn't very often), they ate fatty foods. They had a natural liking for sweet tastes, which helped them choose ripe fruits, for example, over green ones. (Ripe foods have more nutrients than unripe foods.) When their bodies were able to store extra calories and nutrients as fat, they could survive times of famine.

When food supplies were stable, hunter-gatherers naturally provided their bodies with the nutrients that were necessary for good health. When food was scarce or important food groups

THE PROOF'S IN THE POOP

At Oregon's Paisley Caves, archaeologist Dennis L. Jenkins and his team uncovered evidence of hunter-gatherer diets from about 14,300 years ago. In addition to the butchered bones of ancient horses and camels, the excavations yielded one stone tool that could have been used to smash bones to get at the fatty marrow inside. Most important and exciting, however, was the discovery of fossilized human feces (poop). The archaeologists know the feces are human in origin because they tested the DNA. The analysis helped them to learn about the diets of some of the earliest inhabitants of North America. The feces contained chipmunk and squirrel bones, bison hair, fish scales, protein related to dogs and birds, and plant residue from grass and sunflowers. At other archaeological sites in the United States, fecal evidence suggests that hunter-gatherer diets are just as varied. Some of the foods eaten include cactus, muskrat, wild onions, persimmons, and beetles.

were unavailable, disease and starvation were likely. However, our ancestors had one advantage over modern humans: They could not forage and hunt for non-nutritional foods. They could not dig up French fries from the earth or spear a cupcake.

MODERN DIETS

In some ways, modern humans face nutritional disadvantages that our ancestors did not. We still crave fats and sugars, so if they are easily available, we eat too much of them. In many parts of the world, people no longer face feast-famine cycles, but still often eat (and store nutrients in their cells) as though a famine is coming. In other parts of the world, humans cope with political, social, and ecological situations that leave them unable to eat nutritiously. In much of the world, foods are often no longer available fresh from the earth or in a natural state. They are grown in depleted soil, processed and altered to make them cheap and palatable, raised to be fat and tender, and often stripped of their nutrients. Perhaps because of dislike or childhood habits or personal beliefs, many people also refuse to eat vegetables or any animal products, or anything but processed foods. When diets are too restricted, they are likely to be low in many nutrients.

A varied diet is no longer a part of the lifestyle of many modern humans. This has been true since people abandoned hunter-gatherer lifestyles and began living in cities and towns. Nutritional disease and deficiencies have been the inevitable result. It is not the starvation that hunter-gatherers risked in times of famine. It is not the short life spans that early humans faced because of diseases, injuries, and body breakdowns when sufficient food was not available. The effects of a nutritionally deficient diet in modern humans are not always dramatically apparent, although around the world millions of people still face the terrible problem of insufficient food.

More and more, scientists and researchers are realizing that nutrient deficiencies cause or exacerbate many modern diseases.

Optimum health cannot exist unless all the nutrients needed for cells to function are available, but it has taken centuries of experience and study to define this optimal nutrition, to understand what goes wrong that leads to disease, and to avoid the disease process altogether. Some nutritional strategies to prevent disease were known before specific nutrients were identified. Others are suspected, but not yet proven. Still others are yet to be discovered.

REVIEW

Nutrition is the sum total of the interaction between the foods we eat and how our bodies use and process the nourishing substances in the foods. There are six classes of nutrients: carbohydrates, proteins, fats, vitamins, minerals, and water. Macronutrients are fats, some minerals, proteins, carbohydrates, and water. They are required by the body in large amounts. Micronutrients include vitamins and some minerals. They are required in small amounts. Both macronutrients and micronutrients are needed for good health and to prevent disease. Through the process of metabolism, the nutrients in foods are made available to the body's trillions of cells. Each cell is able to perform its work by breaking down and building up specific nutrients so that they can be used for energy, as cell building blocks, and to regulate cell function. Modern diets are often deficient in one or more nutrients, and these deficiencies lead to cell dysfunction. Scientists are still learning about the complex relationship between nutrients and the prevention of disease.

2

DEFICIENCY DISEASES

About 10,000 years ago, humans began to make the transition from eating the wild foods that nourished hunter-gatherers to eating foods from farming and ranching. This agricultural revolution had many advantages, including a population explosion and the establishment of towns and eventually cities. Still, it had disadvantages, too. Writing in the *Cambridge History of Medicine*, Kenneth F. Kiple says that the agricultural revolution led to a reduction in food diversity, compared with the varied diets of hunter-gatherers. This reduction in variety is still seen today, although it is not as extreme as it was thousands of years ago. In the past, people may have had greater quantities of food available to them, but they depended on just a few staple foods to maintain life. Kiple explains that, at the beginning of the agricultural age, humans paid for this restricted diet with stunted growth and nutritional diseases. As nutritional quality declined, the "classic" vitamin and mineral deficiency diseases appeared. According to Kiple, they are diseases caused by the advance of civilization. Thanks to modern science, people living in wealthy countries are rarely plagued by these diseases anymore, but people in poor countries still face the nutritional disadvantages of living in a civilized world.

Vitamin and mineral deficiency diseases are conditions in which the amount of a specific micronutrient in the diet is so low that disability and death occur relatively quickly. As civilization continued to advance, medical practitioners and scientists learned to recognize the symptoms of deficiency diseases and treated them with specific foods, sometimes even before they knew which micronutrients were involved. Vitamins, for example, were not discovered until the twentieth century. Yet, long before that time, a few deficiency diseases could be treated and prevented with nutritional intervention. The different essential vitamins and minerals were identified one by one, as the human need for a wide variety of nutritious foods came to be understood. Each essential micronutrient is associated with its own specific disease and symptoms. Some deficiency diseases are very rare, but others have been common and widespread.

SCURVY AND VITAMIN C

When Europeans first began sea voyages of exploration in the fifteenth century, a strange malady often sickened and killed crews. These sailors had a lack of energy, bleeding gums, loose teeth, swelling of the limbs, large purple marks on the skin (caused by bleeding into muscles), shortness of breath, heart palpitations, and finally jaundice (a yellowing of the skin and eyes), fever, convulsions, and death. Their disease was named scurvy, and it was caused by the depletion of vitamin C from their bodies because of their limited diets aboard ship. Vitamin C is a **water-soluble** vitamin, meaning that it cannot be stored in the fat cells of the body. It needs to be ingested every day; after about 30 days, any stored vitamin C in the body is used up. Fresh foods—such as fruits that contain vitamin C—were not available; the typical seaman's diet consisted exclusively of cured, salted meat and hard biscuits. No one, however, suspected that nutrition was the cause of scurvy. It

TABLE 2.1 VITAMIN DEFICIENCY DISEASES (NOT INCLUDING RARE DEFICIENCIES)

Vitamin	Deficiency Disease	Symptoms	Food Sources
Vitamin A	Xerophthalmia	Drying of tear ducts, ulcers of the cornea, blindness	Liver, eggs, orange and yellow fruits and vegetables, dark green leafy vegetables
Vitamin D	Rickets (in children) and osteomalacia (in adults)	Bone malformation, bowed legs, bone pain, weakness	Fortified foods, such as milk; cod liver oil
Vitamin C	Scurvy	Bleeding gums, hemorrhaging, weakness, fatigue, edema, slow wound healing	Citrus fruits, berries, green peppers, melons, potatoes, tomatoes
Thiamine (vitamin B1)	Beriberi	Muscle weakness and wasting, mental confusion, anorexia, nerve damage	Whole grains, liver
Riboflavin (vitamin B2)	[No disease name; always accompanied by other vitamin deficiencies.]	Purple tongue, mouth ulcers, cracked mouth corners, sore throat, skin breakdowns	Milk, leafy vegetables, eggs, meat, soybeans, wheat bran

Vitamin	Deficiency Disease	Symptoms	Food Sources
Niacin (vitamin B3)	Pellagra	Vomiting, diarrhea, depression, skin rashes, fatigue, memory loss, disorientation	Meats, beans
Pyridoxine (vitamin B6)	B6 Deficiency	Skin disorders, anemia, convulsions	Meats, whole grains, nuts, beans
Folic acid or folate (vitamin B9)	Folic acid deficiency, anemia	Fatigue, weakness, fainting, anorexia, headache, irritability, trouble breathing	Leafy vegetables, liver, orange juice, beans, wheat germ
Vitamin B12	Pernicious anemia	Immature red blood cells, nerve damage, memory loss, disorientation, dementia, vision problems, insomnia, loss of bladder and bowel control	Animal products (vegans may need supplements)

Adapted from "Micronutrients in Health and Disease," "Table 2: Vitamin Functions, Deficiency Diseases, Toxicity Symptoms, and Dietary Reference Intakes," NutritionMD. Available Online. URL: http://www.nutritionmd.org/health_care_providers/general_nutrition/micro_table2.html

was believed to be an infection, passed from person to person, and one from which almost no one recovered.

In 1746, ship's doctor James Lind conducted one of the world's first controlled experiments in an effort to discover a treatment for scurvy. After 10 weeks at sea, 80 of the 350 sailors aboard his

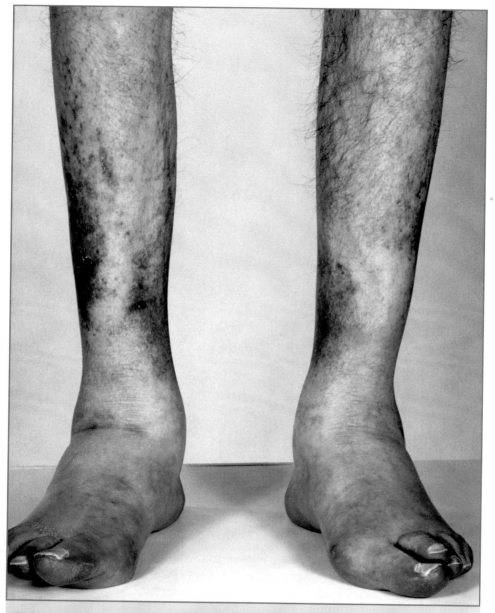

FIGURE 2.1 Scurvy is caused by a deficiency in vitamin C, which is essential to the body's production of collagen—the connective tissue that holds together skin, bones, muscles, organs, and nervous system. Symptoms of this disease include bleeding gums, swelling of limbs, hard bumps on the leg muscles, and red spots around the hair follicles on the legs and other areas.

ship were suffering with the disease. Lind chose 12 of them and subjected them to 6 treatments that were often recommended in folklore as helpful against scurvy. Lind ordered two men to drink a quart of cider a day. Two drank half a pint of seawater every day. Two were dosed with spoonfuls of vinegar. Two more were given doses of a "tonic" that included mustard seed, nutmeg, and garlic three times a day, as well as being purged (given laxatives plus medicine to induce vomiting in order to "clean out" the body) by the doctor on a daily basis. Two men were fed a medicine of the time that Lind identified as "elixir vitriol"—a concoction that included, among other ingredients, alcohol and sulfuric acid. And the last two men were given two oranges and a lemon each day for six days (at which time the supply was gone).

The two men who had been given oranges and lemons made dramatic recoveries. Lind had discovered how to cure—or prevent—scurvy, although he still did not know that nutritional deficiency was the cause. He continued to believe that the disease was caused by the humidity at sea. Nevertheless, in 1795, the British Admiralty issued a requirement that all seamen on its ships must be issued a daily ration of lime juice. This order ended scurvy in the British navy and gave British sailors the nickname "Limeys." Limeys were lucky. It has been estimated that at least one million people died of scurvy by the end of the nineteenth century. They were sailors, explorers, prison inmates, institutionalized patients—any people without access to fresh fruits and vegetables. All of their symptoms were the result of a breakdown in the collagen in their bodies. Vitamin C is essential to the production of collagen, the connective tissue that holds together our skin, bones, muscles, organs, and nervous systems. It also helps the body's cells to use other essential vitamins and minerals.

DISCOVERING VITAMINS AND CURING BERIBERI

Not until the twentieth century did the world understand that certain "factors" in foods were necessary to healthy body functioning. In 1912, these first-recognized factors were named "vitamines" by the Polish scientist Cashmir Funk, because they were "vital" to life. In 1928, scientists finally isolated the factor in citrus and other fresh foods—vitamin C, or ascorbic acid—that prevented scurvy. In 1929, Sir Frederick Gowland Hopkins, a British chemist, received a Nobel Prize for work that proved that essential nutrients existed in foods and were necessary for health and growth. He shared the prize with Christiaan Eijkman, a Danish scientist who had found the cause of beriberi, a vitamin deficiency disease that killed thousands around the world.

Beriberi is caused by a deficiency in vitamin B1, also known as thiamine. Symptoms include muscle weakness, lameness and paralysis, edema (fluid buildup), pain, fever, and finally heart failure, psychosis, and death. Beriberi first came to the attention of Europeans when they began ocean exploration and colonization of Asia. The Dutch were the major seafarers of time. During the

STARVING FOR POTATOES

Between 1845 and 1851, a fungal disease called blight struck the potato crops in Ireland, resulting in almost total crop failures as potatoes rotted in the fields. The Great Potato Famine, as it came to be called, was a disaster because the laborers and poor peasants of Ireland were almost completely dependent upon potatoes as their main source of food. It has been estimated that a typical working man in Ireland at the time ate 14 pounds (6.3 kilograms) of potatoes every day. Without potatoes to eat, more than one million Irish died. They starved to death or succumbed to scurvy, pellagra, and beriberi, as well as the "famine diseases" of cholera and typhus that attack weakened bodies. Potatoes provided about 80% of the calories of the Irish poor. They were the only source of vitamin C in the Irish diet. They also provided the B vitamins that prevented beriberi and pellagra.

seventeenth century, they established the Dutch East India Company. Over the centuries, the company became a multinational corporation with the goals of trading, establishing colonies, and settling in China, Sri Lanka, Indonesia, and the Pacific Islands. Often, the Europeans were struck down by a terrible, mysterious disease, one already well-known to native populations. Sri Lankans gave beriberi the name we know today; it is a Singhalese word meaning "I cannot." It was a reference to the inability to walk or even think clearly due to the total breakdown of the body.

By the nineteenth century, beriberi was epidemic among European settlers in many parts of Asia and the Pacific. It was rampant in Indonesia. It had become the scourge of the Japanese navy, too. Yet, the poorest members of indigenous populations did not get the disease; it seemed to single out the "civilized," urban, well-off people instead. It was indeed a disease of civilization, a result of eating white rice. White rice has been polished to remove the husk,

In an effort to alleviate the suffering in Ireland, the British government bought shipments of corn to be distributed to the starving people. Soup kitchens provided gruel made with cornmeal and rice, with perhaps one slice of bread. By 1847, scurvy became an epidemic. Doctors were shocked to find "sea-scurvy" occurring in the countryside. They coined a new name for the disease—"land scurvy." Medical researchers theorized that the scurvy was somehow related to the potato crop failure, but few understood that grains, which provide no vitamin C, were no substitute for potatoes. No recognition of B vitamin deficiency disease existed. More people died of nutritional diseases than died of actual starvation. By the time the potato famine ended, Ireland had lost one-quarter of its people, either to death or to immigration spurred by the need to escape the famine.

or bran. The bran contains thiamine. The poorest people ate a diet consisting mostly of rice, too, but they could not afford white rice. They had to eat brown rice, which still had the thiamine-containing bran. This protected them from beriberi.

CHICKENS TO THE RESCUE

In 1886, the Dutch East India Company sent Eijkman, a medical doctor, to Indonesia to search for the "germ" or supposed parasite that caused beriberi. Eijkman spent 11 years failing at the task, and finally was given the answer by a flock of chickens. One day, as he happened to walk by a chicken coop, Eijkman noticed that the chickens looked like they had beriberi. Their wings hung loosely, and they stumbled around on feet that looked twisted and paralyzed. A few weeks later, they had mysteriously recovered. The chickens lived in the compound where Eijkman had his laboratory and were fed by the cook. Eijkman questioned the cook and discovered that the previous cook had run out of the cheap brown rice that the chickens usually were fed. So he fed them white rice instead. The new cook refused to waste expensive white rice on chickens, and fed them only brown rice. It was the clue Eijkman needed. With further experiments, he discovered that brown rice prevented beriberi in chickens. (This was also true, Eijkman and other scientists later discovered, of beans, lentils, and any whole-grain cereal.) Eijkman did not know what the "active principle" was that prevented beriberi, but he did hypothesize that it was a nutrient in food.

Thiamine was the first vitamin to be identified during the 1920s. Today, scientists know that it is essential for building an enzyme in the body that is used to produce energy from glucose, and for converting glucose to fat so that it can be stored. Without any thiamine in the diet, muscles, nerves, and the digestive system break down, and beriberi develops in about 30 days. People need only about 1 or 2 milligrams of thiamine a day to prevent beriberi. (One milligram equals about 0.03 ounces.) This small

FIGURE 2.2 Dutch doctor Christiaan Eijkman discovered that brown rice prevented beriberi in chickens after hypothesizing that the birds' recovery must be because of a nutrient in the food. The answer turned out to be the vitamin thiamine, which is essential for building an enzyme in the body that is used to produce energy from glucose and for converting glucose to fat so that it can be stored.

quantity of thiamine protects people in wealthy countries from disease and death from beriberi, mostly because it is routinely added to many of the processed foods we eat, such as white bread and polished rice, in a process called **fortification** or enrichment. This process returns the thiamine that was lost when the grain was milled and the husk removed.

VITAMIN D AND RICKETS

Fortification stopped another vitamin deficiency in wealthy countries during the twentieth century. The disease was rickets, and its primary cause was a lack of vitamin D. Beginning in the seventeenth century, rickets was epidemic among poor children living in crowded, dirty, industrial cities, especially northern ones. At the end of the nineteenth century, one study of children in two cities in the Netherlands and the United States reported that 80% to 90% of the children had rickets. These children experienced a softening of their bones, increased risk of bone fractures, misshapen ribs, and deformities of legs that bowed under the weights of their bodies. Without enough vitamin D, they could not properly absorb calcium, the major building block of strong bones. If rickets progressed unchecked, the children died, because calcium also is essential for the functioning of other body tissues, such as the brain and intestines.

Vitamin D is known as the sunshine vitamin because it can be absorbed through the skin from the sun's rays. However, winter sunshine is weak. Winter weather often keeps children inside, and winter storms produce clouds that block the sun. Even in summer, industrial cities in the past were so polluted that little sunshine reached children living in dark, crowded tenements and slums. Children with darker skin also absorb vitamin D from the sun less efficiently than paler children. Few foods are a source of vitamin D. Vitamin D from the sun is metabolized by and stored in the liver. It is **fat soluble**, so it could be obtained from cod liver oil, but few children were offered this "tonic" until the 1930s. That

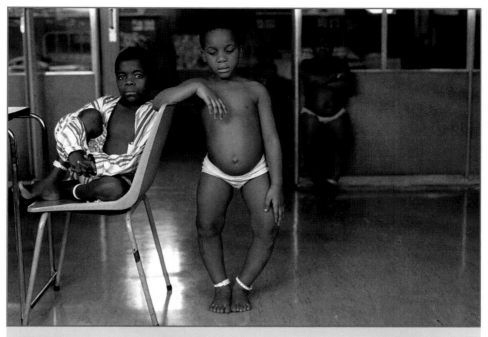

FIGURE 2.3 These children in a hospital in Soweto, South Africa, suffer from rickets. Rickets is caused by a vitamin D deficiency; the body cannot properly absorb calcium without it. Those with the disease can experience softening of bones, misshaped ribs, and legs that bow under the weight of the body.

is when the connection between sunshine, vitamin D, and rickets was finally understood. By the 1940s, milk was routinely fortified with vitamin D, and infants were given cod liver oil daily. In wealthier, industrialized countries, rickets was all but eradicated.

NIACIN AND PELLAGRA

The 1930s saw efforts to eradicate another vitamin deficiency disease—one that was especially rampant in southern regions of the United States. It was pellagra, caused by the combination of a low-protein diet and a lack of vitamin B3 (niacin). Dr. V. P. Sydenstricker, writing in *The American Journal of Clinical Nutri-*

tion, calls pellagra "a manmade disease" because it results from dependence on corn as a dietary staple. Pellagra usually occurred among people who could not afford to buy meats, eggs, or milk. The disease was also epidemic in institutions such as orphanages, mental hospitals, and prisons, where cheap foods were a priority. The problem was that the corn was heavily processed and milled so that the hull, with its niacin, was gone. People lived on corn-meal, grits, cornstarch, and perhaps some pork fat and greens.

Without niacin in the diet, most cell metabolism fails. Niacin can be manufactured by the body, but only if certain amino acids are available in the diet. Poor or institutionalized people, with neither niacin nor these amino acids, suffered the "4 Ds": diarrhea (accompanied by nausea and inability to eat), dermatitis (skin breakdowns and red rashes), dementia (insanity), and death (usually due to heart failure). In the early twentieth century in the United States, about 100,000 people came down with it each year, and 10,000 died. By 1930, about 200,000 people got the disease each year and about one in every three people with pellagra died from it.

During the 1930s, scientists and medical doctors came to understand the role that nutrition played in the onset of many diseases, but for years they could not find the factor that cured pellagra. They discovered that certain foods, such as liver and yeast, could be effective in treating the disease, but because their pellagra patients often vomited up any food, their efforts at treatment frequently failed. During the search to isolate the "anti-pellagra vitamin," researchers discovered other B vitamins—B6 and riboflavin. However, it was not until 1937 that a research team isolated and purified niacin. In 1938, researchers discovered that riboflavin cured pellagra patients of the skin conditions (the dermatitis) that accompanied pellagra. By the 1940s, with the poverty of the Great Depression at an end, white flour, corn meal, grits, and white rice all were fortified or enriched with B vitamins. Pellagra was a killer no more.

THE MINERAL FOR THE THYROID GLAND

The first half of the twentieth century saw an end to many micro-nutrient deficiency diseases in wealthy countries, and mineral deficiency diseases were no exception. Iodine, for instance, is a somewhat rare kind of salt that occurs in seawater and in the soil, air, and fresh water in coastal regions. Where it occurs naturally, plants absorb the iodine from the soil. Animals and people who eat the plants or drink the water ingest iodine. Once absorbed, iodine travels through the bloodstream and is used by the thyroid gland in the neck as an essential part of hormone production. These hormones control the rate at which cellular metabolism occurs throughout the body, and they ensure the smooth functioning of nerve cells and body growth.

Without iodine, the thyroid gland malfunctions, and two terrible diseases result. Goiter is the swelling of the thyroid gland as it struggles to produce hormones without enough iodine. People with goiters have large, disfiguring lumps on the sides of their necks. In severe cases, the thyroid gland cannot function. Affected people suffer with fatigue, dry skin, chills, depression, and mental slowness. If a pregnant woman is severely deficient in iodine, her fetus is badly affected. The child is born with a birth defect known as cretinism. He or she has a goiter and is severely mentally retarded, has stunted growth, and is often deaf.

In 1922, a region of the American Midwest was known as the "goiter belt" because the incidence of goiter was so high there. Goiter and cretinism were also epidemic in Switzerland, and for the same reasons. Both areas are far from oceans, and that means they are far from naturally occurring iodine. In that year, pediatrician David Cowie of Michigan organized the Iodized Salt Committee of the Michigan State Medical Society. On the basis of previous medical research, it urged the voluntary addition of iodine to table salt. By 1924, the committee's efforts were a success, and iodized table salt was sold in stores, advertised as a benefit to the public health. In Switzerland, the year 1922 was pivotal,

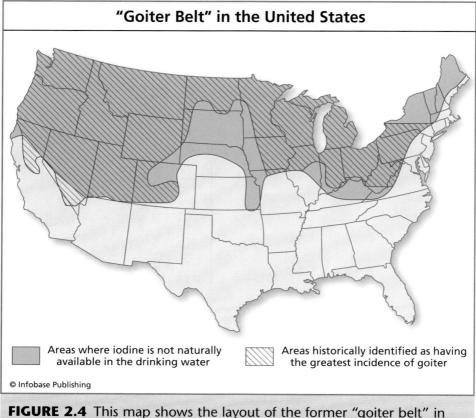

"Goiter Belt" in the United States

Areas where iodine is not naturally available in the drinking water

Areas historically identified as having the greatest incidence of goiter

© Infobase Publishing

FIGURE 2.4 This map shows the layout of the former "goiter belt" in the northern United States and the areas in which the iodine content of drinking water is naturally low.

too. The Swiss Commission of Goiter was established, and on its recommendation, salt was required to be iodized throughout the country.

IODINE DEFICIENCY TODAY

In both the U.S. goiter belt and in Switzerland, the incidence of goiter and cretinism dropped dramatically. Gradually, because of iodized salt, both goiters caused by iodine deficiency and cretinism disappeared throughout much of the world. Yet, despite scientific knowledge, iodine deficiency is not a disease of the past. Neither are other mineral and vitamin deficiency diseases, although the ability to prevent all these diseases has existed for decades. In poorer countries, many of these diseases are still rampant. For example, about 13% of the world's population suffers with iodine deficiency and goiter. Most of them live in Africa, the Middle East, China, and South America. In 1996, scientists estimated that at least 10 million people in China were mentally retarded because of iodine deficiency. In 2006, iodine deficiency remained the top preventable cause of mental retardation throughout the world, affecting some 20 million children. The problem is not one of nutritional information, but one of poverty and lack of governmental prevention efforts in poor countries.

FIGURE 2.5 Due to poverty and lack of governmental prevention efforts, poor countries such as Bangladesh, where the woman shown here lives, have many cases of goiter and iodine deficiency.

CLASSIC DEFICIENCY DISEASES IN THE MODERN WORLD

In 2004, the United Nations International Children's Emergency Fund (UNICEF) established a yearly global reporting system on the prevalence of nutritional deficiencies. It states that one-third of the world's population suffers from vitamin and/or mineral deficiencies. Half of all children with a vitamin or mineral deficiency suffer not one deficiency, but multiple deficiencies. Micronutrient deficiencies are particularly damaging to children because their

THE WORLD'S MOST COMMON DEFICIENCY DISORDER

Iron is an essential mineral that is used to produce hemoglobin—the protein in red blood cells that carries oxygen throughout the body and gives blood its red color. When iron is deficient in the body, hemoglobin cannot be produced, red blood cells are small and pale, and iron-deficiency anemia develops. Iron deficiency is the most common cause of anemia. Symptoms include paleness, fatigue, rapid heart rate, irritability, and a sore, swollen tongue. Iron-deficiency anemia can develop either because the diet is low in iron or because the body has an increased need for iron. Increased need may be the result of rapid growth, such as when children and teens go through growth spurts, or when women are pregnant or breastfeeding an infant. Loss of blood also can lead to a loss of iron and anemia. This situation may occur with menstruation in women or because of injury or undiagnosed internal bleeding, especially in the gastrointestinal tract. Iron-deficiency anemia is easily diagnosed with a blood test that measures the number of red blood cells in the bloodstream and, assuming an injury is not the cause, it is easily treated with iron supplements. Foods providing iron include meats, leafy greens, lima beans, black-eyed peas, pinto beans, eggs, and iron-fortified breads. Oysters and beef liver are particularly rich in iron.

bodies and brains are growing rapidly and because the lack of specific nutrients makes it difficult for them to fight off common diseases. For example, UNICEF reports that 140 million children under the age of 6 suffer vitamin A deficiency, the leading cause of blindness in 118 countries. A deficiency in the mineral zinc causes the deaths of 800,000 children each year because their bodies cannot fight off infections. A deficiency of iron in the diet kills about 50,000 young women a year because they hemorrhage (bleed excessively) during childbirth.

Classic vitamin deficiency diseases have not disappeared from the developing world, either. Outbreaks of pellagra, beriberi, and rickets continue wherever people have severely restricted diets. For example, an outbreak of beriberi occurred in a prison in the Philippines in 2009. About 40 prisoners came down with beriberi due to a cheap, unvaried diet of polished rice, dried fish, and squash or sweet potato soup. In Thailand, in 2005, a group of 15 fishermen developed beriberi after two months at sea eating nothing but seafood and polished rice. Two of them died.

In Ulan Bator, Mongolia, the government's Health Authority reported in 2009 that rickets, especially among infants, was a major problem. About 40% of newborn babies in this capital city were estimated to be at risk for rickets. One reason these babies are vulnerable is the traditional practice of swaddling infants, which means that little skin is exposed to the sun. Medical scientists say that where children are kept indoors, covered in clothing, or living in smoggy, industrial cities, the risk of rickets is high.

Pellagra is endemic in poor countries where diets are high in corn and low in protein, including parts of Africa, China, India, and Indonesia. No one knows the incidence of pellagra in the world, but the largest documented epidemic in modern times occurred in Angola between 1999 and 2002, in the town of Kuito. Due to a civil war, refugees in the town had little food, especially high-protein food. A total of 3,859 cases of pellagra were identified by the relief agency Médecins Sans Frontières (Doctors without Borders). In 2008, in Zimbabwe, a news report claimed that

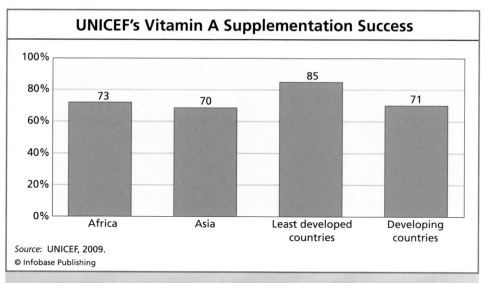

FIGURE 2.6 This graph shows the percentage of children 6 months to 4 years and 9 months old (59 months old) given two doses of vitamin A by UNICEF in 2008. The information represents work in 59 countries that have national programs.

400 inmates out of 1,300 in a Harare prison died of pellagra after being fed a diet consisting only of cabbage and sadza (cornmeal). Although epidemics of pellagra are rare, pockets of poverty and refugee crises in the developing world mean that niacin deficiency continues to claim victims.

TO PREVENT DEFICIENCY DISEASES

Vitamins and minerals are cheap. In wealthy countries, both are routinely added to foods. UNICEF estimates that such fortification of staple foods in developing countries would cost only a few cents per person per year. Fortification of foods such as flour, sugar, cooking oil, and salt would eradicate micronutrient deficiency diseases in much of the world. UNICEF says that the solution to the problem involves governments making it a priority to require food

TABLE 2.2 PROFILE OF SELECTED MICRONUTRIENT DEFICIENCIES IN HAITI

Population	9,296,000
Mortality rate of children under age 5:	80 per 1,000
Vitamin A deficiency in children 6 to 59 months old	32%
Iodine deficiency	58.9%
Prevalence of anemia in children 6 to 59 months	60.6%
Prevalence of anemia in women	45.8%

Source: www.micronutrient.org, 2010.

fortification. It has partnered with many poor nations to achieve this goal. In addition, global relief organizations and governments can provide cheap vitamin supplements to vulnerable people. For example, in cooperation with UNICEF, 40 poor countries now provide at least 70% of their children with at least one vitamin A capsule per year. This small amount is not really adequate, but since the inception of UNICEF's Micronutrient Initiative in 2004, it has saved the eyesight of "hundreds of thousands" of children, says the Global Progress Report. In addition, iodine deficiency has been halved around the world. In places such as Angola, relief organizations administer vitamin supplements and enriched diets in order to save the lives of people with pellagra. The solution to vitamin and mineral deficiency diseases is simple, yet one-third of the world's population still suffers with them. UNICEF says, "The challenge is therefore clear. And when so much could be achieved for so many and for so little, it would be a matter of global disgrace if vitamin and mineral deficiency were not brought under control in the years immediately ahead."

REVIEW

Classic vitamin and mineral deficiency diseases occur when the intake of a specific micronutrient is so low that serious illness is the result. Until the essential vitamins and minerals were discovered and isolated during the first half of the twentieth century, scientists did not understand the relationship between nutrition and disease. Epidemics of diseases occurred as the result of eating a restricted diet that led to deficiency in one or more micronutrient. Each micronutrient is linked to a specific disease. For example, a lack of vitamin C causes scurvy; a severe deficiency of vitamin D leads to rickets; a failure to ingest different B vitamins causes pellagra or beriberi. Mineral deficiencies cause diseases such as goiter, cretinism, and anemia. Today, these diseases are virtually eradicated in wealthy countries, due to scientific knowledge and the fortification and enrichment of foods. However, vitamin and mineral deficiency diseases continue to plague the developing world. Global initiatives to provide enriched staple foods and vitamin supplements to people in poor countries are ongoing.

3

UNDERNUTRITION

As devastating as micronutrient deficiencies can be, a more serious problem is undernutrition. Undernutrition is a type of malnutrition or starvation caused by a deficit in calories, protein or both. It also is called **protein energy malnutrition (PEM)**. In 2008, in the medical journal *The Lancet*, researchers estimated that undernutrition is responsible for 2.2 million deaths each year in children under five. Médecins Sans Frontières (Doctors without Borders) puts the number of deaths at 5 million children per year.

PEM AND THE BODY

A person getting too few calories is likely to be getting too few micronutrients as well, but PEM has extreme consequences. Not getting the calories it needs, the body first breaks down fat to use for energy. Then, it begins to break down muscle and organ tissue. If the situation continues long enough, organ death and

Malnutrition Hotspots

The shaded countries have a high mortality rate (greater than 50 per 1,000) for children under five years old as well as a greater than 30% of stunting[1] in under-fives.

EUROPE

ASIA

AFRICA

AUSTRALIA

Note: This legend represents wasting[2] in population of children under five years old in these countries.

Countries with more than 15% acute malnutrition[3]

Countries with more than 10% acute malnutrition[4]

Countries with more than 4% acute malnutrition[5]

Countries with the most children under five years old with severe acute malnutrition. (Estimates in millions)

India	8.0
Democratic Republic of the Congo	1.7
Pakistan	1.2
Nigeria	1.1
Ethiopia	0.6

[1] Stunting—Growth retardation, indicated by low height for age (height for age according to WHO 2005 Growth Standards).

[2] Wasting—Emaciation or thinness as measured by low weight for one's height according to WHO 2005 Growth Standards).

[3] Burkina Faso, Chad, Democratic Republic of the Congo, Eritrea, India, Lao People's Democratic Republic, Madagascar, Mauritania, Sudan, Yemen.

[4] Bangladesh, Central African Republic, Comoros, Ethiopia, Guinea, Guinea-Bissau, Haiti, Mali, Myanmar, Namibia, Nepal, Niger, Nigeria, Pakistan, Sierra Leone, Somalia, Timor-Leste, Togo.

[5] Afghanistan, Angola, Benin, Burundi, Cambodia, Cameroon, Democratic Republic of the Congo, Côte d'Ivoire, Equatorial Guinea, Ghana, Iraq, Kenya, Democratic People's Republic of Korea, Liberia, Malawi, Mozambique, Rwanda, Tanzania, Uganda, Zambia, Zimbabwe.

Sources: Population Reference Bureau 2007 World Population Data. WHO analyses of national nutritional surveys done 2001–2006. UNICEF—The State of the World's Children 2008.

© Infobase Publishing

FIGURE 3.1 The countries shaded on this map have high mortality rates due to malnutrition for children under five.

death by starvation are the result. Without the protein intake needed to build body cells, the same organ malfunction and death can occur. Although anyone of any age can suffer from acute protein energy malnutrition, it is particularly devastating for children who do not have access to enough food. Their growth and development are severely, and often permanently, affected. They cannot fight off the most minor infections, and are likely to die. Undernutrition is usually a problem among the very poor in developing countries. Dr. Simon Rabinowitz, a medical expert on undernutrition, estimates that 50% of children in Asia are malnourished, as are 30% in Africa and 20% in Latin America. However, undernutrition also can occur among certain populations in wealthy countries.

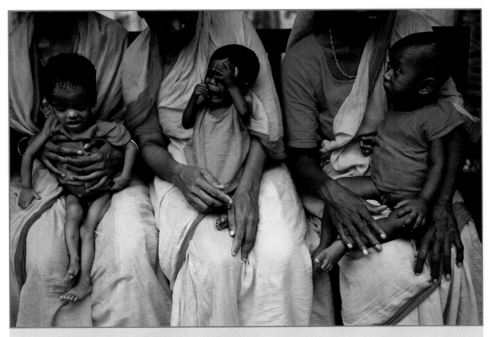

FIGURE 3.2 Protein energy malnutrition (PEM), or undernutrition, has extreme and devastating consequences, especially for children who do not have enough food. The two Bangladeshi children on the left are malnourished and suffer from diarrhea; the child on the right recovered with a proper diet in a research hospital in Bangladesh.

MARASMUS

PEM takes two main forms. Marasmus is the disease caused by a deficit in calories and energy. Although it is primarily caused by too little food, or a negative energy balance, it also may occur because the food eaten is not being absorbed and metabolized, such as in the case of prolonged vomiting and diarrhea. Children with a negative energy balance are less active, lethargic, grow slowly, lose weight, and have a slowed metabolism.

As the deficit continues, the victim becomes emaciated. The brain, skeleton, and kidneys consume energy at high rates, and these organs receive available nutrients first. The pancreas, digestive tract, liver, and heart begin to break down. Muscles begin to waste away as the body breaks them down for energy. Then, bones stop growing. The thyroid gland begins to shrink, and a condition called hypothyroidism develops. This means that the thyroid gland is not producing hormones in the right quantity, and so the

ANOREXIA NERVOSA

Anorexia nervosa is a medical and psychological disorder that leads to self-starvation through extreme dieting and exercise. An individual affected by this eating disorder may become emaciated and yet continue to believe that he or she is too fat. Severe protein energy malnutrition (PEM) is a likely outcome when the disorder is untreated. An anorexic person with PEM is a true medical emergency. These people require hospitalization and re-feeding treatment, in addition to long-term residential treatment and/or psychological intervention so that they can return to eating a normal diet. Although the disorder is treatable, the physical symptoms and dangers are the same as with any case of PEM, and the risk of death from heart failure is significant. Even when health is regained, permanent damage can result, such as stunted growth or heart problems.

signals to the body to regulate growth, temperature, and brain and heart function fail. The heart enlarges, and brain functioning may be disabled.

BODILY DEVASTATION

Multiple vitamin and mineral deficiency symptoms appear, and the body's **immune system** becomes impaired. The immune system is the complex way the body protects itself against disease. The body stops producing enough germ-fighting cells such as T cells, which seek out and destroy foreign invaders. The **antibody** called immunoglobulin A (IgA) also is severely deficient. IgA is a protein, as are all antibodies, and is made by the immune system in response to foreign proteins, such as bacteria. IgA is found in areas of the body with mucous membranes, such as in the mouth, eyes, and intestines. When it is deficient, infections easily attack and take hold, particularly in the digestive system, because the few antibodies available are overwhelmed by infectious invaders.

If an infection does not kill the child, he or she begins to look shrunken and wasted. Even facial fat disappears. Finally, the essential organs, such as the brain, are affected, and the child may become permanently mentally impaired. When marasmus is at its most severe, the child characteristically resembles an elderly person, loses interest in his or her surroundings, is apathetic and unresponsive, and according to observers, seems to be lying still and waiting for death. The mortality rate for children with marasmus, even with medical intervention, can be as high as 30%. According to the World Health Organization (WHO), marasmus is a serious problem around the world. The WHO estimates that it affects some 50 million children in the first five years of life.

MARASMUS IN WEALTHY COUNTRIES

In wealthy countries, marasmus usually affects children with chronic diseases, institutionalized children, or those who are neglected or abused. For example, a child with cystic fibrosis— a genetic disease that causes an increased calorie need and poor absorption of nutrients—can easily become malnourished. Without treatment, such a child simply cannot eat enough to maintain normal weight and to grow and develop properly. The child may have a huge appetite, but the body excretes many nutrients because it cannot make the enzymes required for efficient metabolism. Eventually, the child can become emaciated and lose interest in food.

Although it is rare today, in the past, infants in orphanages sometimes exhibited failure to thrive (the first stage of marasmus) because they were not touched and caressed and received no loving emotional support. Such infants often lost interest in food and wasted away. Occasionally, infants subjected to extreme child abuse and neglect in their own homes may develop marasmus, because they are ignored or because they are not offered proper food. The parent may intentionally starve the infant or be so ill or depressed that the baby is left isolated, not parented, and irregularly fed. Most often, such cases occur in the first year of the child's life.

TREATING MARASMUS

Treatment of marasmus is difficult because the person doesn't want to eat, and the digestive system no longer works properly. Dr. Rabinowitz says that prevention is much easier than treatment, which is usually prolonged and complicated in severe cases. Almost always, the treatment is further complicated by the immediate need to treat serious infections. Fluids—carefully balanced with glucose and salt—are the first requirement, because children with marasmus are dehydrated and suffer **electrolyte** imbalances. Often, the fluid solution is provided through a tube that is threaded through the nose and into the stomach. Treatment aims to avoid cardiac failure (from shocking the body with too much, too soon) and to overcome the victim's anorexia so that re-feeding can begin. Feeding is done by mouth or by the tube. The number

TABLE 3.1 HOW STARVATION AFFECTS THE BODY

Area	Effects
Digestive system	Decreased production of stomach acid Shrinking of the stomach Frequent, often fatal, diarrhea
Cardiovascular system (heart and blood vessels)	Reduced heart size, reduced amount of blood pumped, slow heart rate, and low blood pressure Ultimately, heart failure
Respiratory system	Slow breathing and reduced lung capacity Ultimately, respiratory failure
Reproductive system	Reduced size of ovaries and testes Loss of sex drive (libido) Cessation of menstrual periods
Nervous system	Apathy and irritability In children, mental retardation (sometimes) Mental dysfunction, particularly in older people
Muscles	Reduced muscle size and strength, impairing the ability to exercise or work
Blood	Anemia
Metabolism (body processes to convert food into energy or to synthesize needed substances)	Low body temperature (hypothermia) Fluid accumulation in the arms, legs, and abdomen Disappearance of fat
Skin and hair	Thin, dry, inelastic skin Dry, sparse hair that falls out easily
Immune system	Impaired ability to fight infections and repair wounds

Source: From Thomas, David R., MD. "Undernutrition," The Merck Manuals Online Medical Library. Available Online. URL: http://www.merck.com/mmhe/sec12/ch153/ch153a.html.

of calories is slowly increased until each day the child is receiving about 80 calories for every 2.2 pounds (1 kilogram) of body weight. The calories are given in about 12 small meals a day. At first, most of the calories must come from carbohydrates, because fats are poorly absorbed by the damaged metabolic systems, and proteins may cause kidney failure.

As the child improves and starts to recover, calories are increased, eating by mouth is strongly encouraged, vitamin and mineral supplements are provided, and fats and proteins become larger portions of the diet. Rabinowitz explains that emotional support, play with other children, interaction with family, and loving attention are critical to recovery, too. He says that the first smile from a marasmic child is an excellent sign of progress. Once a child with marasmus is a normal weight and is eating properly, he or she is discharged from the hospital or clinic, but follow-up is necessary for at least one month to be sure the child does not relapse. When properly treated, even a child with severe marasmus is likely to recover, as long as adequate calories and nutrition remain available.

KWASHIORKOR

Kwashiorkor, the other major PEM, may require an equally difficult treatment program. Kwashiorkor is a disease of protein malnutrition that usually occurs in poor countries, especially during times of drought, famine, or war. The rare cases of kwashiorkor in wealthy countries are almost always due to child abuse. However, it also is sometimes a problem among institutionalized, disabled adults, such as elderly people confined to nursing homes. *Kwashiorkor* is a term from the African language of Ga. It means "the evil spirit that infects the first child when the second child is born." The name accurately reflects both the age at which kwashiorkor most typically begins (between 1 and 3 years) and the most common trigger of the disease. When a second child is born, the mother stops breastfeeding the first in favor of the newborn infant. The toddler is thus deprived of the protein in the mother's milk. Usually, the weaned child is then fed an extremely poor diet. Although calories are adequate, they are almost exclusively from carbohydrates, such as rice, corn, yams, or cassava; the child receives little or no protein. As might be expected from such a diet, the child with kwashiorkor suffers deficiencies in vitamin A, vitamin C, and the B vitamins, as well as in iron and iodine. It is theorized that a lack of essential fatty acids also plays a role, and some researchers suspect that moldy foods, which are common in tropical countries, might be an important factor. The toxins from mold have to be detoxified by the liver, and too much toxic overload can damage the liver. Children with kwashiorkor always have damaged livers. Most of these children also have parasitic, viral, or bacterial infections, as well as chronic diarrhea.

THE PERIL OF KWASHIORKOR

All of the symptoms of kwashiorkor occur because the body is missing the essential amino acids that are the building blocks it needs for maintaining body structure and function. The defining symptom of kwashiorkor is edema: an accumulation of fluids in the body. The child with kwashiorkor does not appear emaciated, but swollen. The edema usually starts in the feet and ankles and then spreads as the disease progresses. A child with severe kwashiorkor has a swollen belly, puffy cheeks, and swollen hands. Other symptoms include lethargy, fatigue, muscle wasting, flaking skin, and thin, reddish, brittle hair. The child fails to grow and is seriously underweight, although the edema can hide the problem. He or she also is irritable, lifeless, and loses appetite.

Kwashiorkor puts a child in serious danger of death: About 4 of every 10 children with this disease will die of it. Once the disease becomes severe, it is difficult to treat. Even when treatment is successful, the child will never achieve his or her full height.

As with marasmus, treatment begins with rehydration, treatment of infection, restoration of electrolyte balance, vitamin and mineral supplements, and slow feeding. Too much protein cannot be given right away, or the liver might be overloaded and permanently damaged. When kwashiorkor was first recognized as a disease during the 1930s, the death rate was 90%, even among hospitalized children. These deaths often occurred because the victims had metabolisms that were adapted to a starvation diet. When the children were suddenly given lots of healthy food, they could not metabolize it. Instead, they went into shock, suffered from liver failure and kidney failure, and died from heart failure.

PREVENTING PEM

Just as with the treatment of PEM, prevention of kwashiorkor and marasmus is a complex problem. Many severely malnourished children do not fall into one neat PEM category or the other. The third PEM, marasmic kwashiorkor, is the term for children exhibiting symptoms of both diseases. In the real world, it can sometimes be impossible to separate one disease from the other. Nevertheless, the severity and danger of any PEM is well known. In theory, it would seem simple to solve the problem of PEM: provide enough calories for growth and health, with a minimum of 12% of those calories coming from high-quality protein foods and 10% coming from fats. However,

(opposite page) **FIGURE 3.3** Though kwashiorkor is caused by malnutrition, children with this condition appear swollen rather than emaciated. Esinyen Ekuwam, seen here in 2004 at 3 years old, suffers from this condition in Kalapata, Kenya, where a drought ruined production of doom palm. The residents there depend almost completely on this fruit for subsistence, even though it has almost no nutritional value and causes the digestive tract to shut down, leading to swollen bellies and starvation.

in areas of the world with chronic malnutrition, preventing undernutrition is not simple.

The World Health Organization (WHO) estimates that by 2015, malnutrition will affect 17.5% of the world's population. This estimate represents a decrease from about 26.5% in 1990, a decrease due in large part to global efforts to prevent hunger by the WHO and other worldwide relief organizations. However,

THE RIGHT TO FOOD

In 1948, the United Nations issued The Universal Declaration of Human Rights. Article 25 begins, "Everyone has the right to a standard of living adequate for the health and well-being of himself and of his family, including food...." Since that time, this right has been difficult to achieve, but Brazil is one country that is taking the declaration seriously and trying to ensure the right to adequate food for all its citizens. Beginning in 2003, the Brazilian government instituted a variety of programs with the goal of eliminating hunger in the country by 2015. The initiative is called "Fome Zero" ("Starvation's Over"). One of its programs, "Bolsa Familia" ("Family Grant"), provides cash from the government to poor families who will agree to keep their children in school, get their children vaccinated, and submit to regular nutritional monitoring for pregnant women and all children in the family under seven years old. The hope is that education and good health in childhood will permanently end the poverty that causes undernutrition. It will mean that, as adults, these children will be able to get good jobs and earn enough money to support their own families. Fome Zero is already yielding dramatic results. Brazil reports that malnutrition among babies had dropped 75% by 2008. Between 2002 and 2007, rates of hospitalization for malnutrition were reduced by 35%. Among families enrolled in the Bolsa Familia Program, 93% of the children and 82% of the adults were eating three or more meals a day by 2007.

despite the reduction of malnutrition around the world, the incidence of PEM has increased in certain areas of Africa, from 24% to 26.8%. In an effort to prevent chronic malnutrition and hunger, the WHO partners with governments, other United Nations agencies, and international relief organizations to set goals, educate people worldwide about the problem of hunger, suggest possible solutions, and feed those in need.

A major educational goal for the WHO is to encourage mothers to breastfeed their infants for the first year of life, to avoid early protein deficiency. In addition to discouraging early weaning, the WHO also provides information to families about the foods necessary for a weaned child, such as fish, meat, and whole grains. It provides family planning programs and explains birth control, encouraging families to space births far enough apart that each child can be breastfed for the recommended time. It teaches basic sanitation, such as hand washing to prevent infections and discarding moldy foods.

Prevention of infection seems to have a drastic effect on PEM. Scientists have long recognized that an infection can trigger PEM in vulnerable, undernourished children. An infection that causes diarrhea will cause nutrients to pass through the body unabsorbed. Diarrhea also leads to dehydration, as ingested fluids are lost. Infections also can increase the body's need for nutrients. In 2007, researchers O.A. Oyelami and T.A. Ogunlesi compared the incidence of kwashiorkor and diarrhea in the town of Ilesa, Nigeria over two decades. In 1992, a mission hospital in the area began to treat measles (which causes diarrhea) and diarrhea by establishing a diarrhea treatment program. Between 1983 and 1991, no such program was available. Starting in 1992, families were strongly encouraged to bring their children for treatment of diarrhea, and hospital staff members were trained to teach mothers how to prevent and treat diarrhea and its accompanying dehydration at home. By 2002, there was a 70% reduction in hospitalized cases of kwashiorkor. The researchers concluded that this reduction was due to the success of the hospital's diarrhea treatment program.

THERAPEUTIC FOOD

In the Nigerian study, however, cases of marasmus were not reduced by preventing diarrhea. Nothing really takes the place of adequate calories. Where it is not possible for families to provide enough food for their malnourished children, the WHO recommends supplementary feeding of specially formulated foods, distributed for free. Such foods were developed in the late 1990s and are called Ready-to-Use Therapeutic Food (RUTF). The most common RUTF is named Plumpy'nut. It is a high-calorie, energy-dense supplement for the treatment of malnutrition and the prevention of fatal or disabling PEM. Plumpy'nut consists of peanut butter, milk powder, sugar, oil, a protein mix, and added vitamins and minerals. It is a paste that is easy to digest, does not have to be cooked, and can be stored at room temperature for two years without spoiling. Each packet of Plumpy'nut contains 500 calories. The number of packets a child is prescribed is based on a recommended feeding dose of 200 calories per kilogram of body weight per day. For example, a baby who weighs 12 pounds (5.5 kg) would be given two and a half packets a day. A child weighing 26 pounds (12 kg) would receive five packets a day. The Plumpy'nut would be fed in about five meals a day and always before any other foods were offered (except breast milk for an infant). Most distribution of Plumpy'nut is through outpatient care when an undernourished, sick child is brought to a clinic or relief organization. During supplemental feeding with Plumpy'nut, the child is seen every two weeks to check his or her progress. Empty packets are returned to the clinic (to be sure the child ate them) and more packets are given until the child is a normal weight and out of danger. Distributors also have to warn parents that they cannot share the Plumpy'nut with other people who are hungry.

Médecins Sans Frontières (MSF), also called Doctors Without Borders, is one of the major relief organizations working to treat chronic undernutrition and prevent PEM around the world. In 2005, during a drought in Niger, it provided RUTF for 63,000

FIGURE 3.4 Plumpy'nut packets help malnourished children get the nutrients they are severely lacking. The packets are filled with an easy-to-digest paste made of peanut butter, milk powder, sugar, oil, protein mix, and added vitamins and minerals.

children. Niger, according to MSF, suffers regular starvation as people run out of their previous year's crop supply and wait for the current year's harvest. MSF refers to this as the hunger gap period, and it can lead to PEM and death for thousands of children. Using RUTF, MSF was able to cure even children with poor appetites and acute malnutrition and saved 91% of the children in the area from PEM. Nevertheless, MSF argues that malnutrition is a neglected global crisis. The WHO agrees, stating that 178 million children worldwide are malnourished. In 2008, MSF pointed out that only 3% of the 20 million acutely malnourished children get the food and treatment they need.

THE RIGHT NUTRIENTS TO STOP PEM

The United States is the biggest donor of food aid in the world, and regularly supplies fortified staple foods, such as flour and vegetable oil, to poor countries to prevent malnutrition. Yet, foods with a few added micronutrients are not enough. Therapeutic foods such as Plumpy'nut are the best foods because they contain powdered milk. MSF asserts that all children need animal products (meat, dairy foods, eggs) if their bodies and minds are to be to be adequately nourished. Animal foods are more expensive than staples fortified with vitamins and minerals.

In 2006, MSF began a policy of providing at least some animal foods to every child it treats for malnutrition. This meant 150,000 children in 22 countries. MSF did not have enough RUTF to feed all the children in need. It estimates that about $5 billion each year would be necessary to prevent and treat chronic malnutrition everywhere in the world with RUTF. MSF considers this need one of the "Top Ten Humanitarian Crises" of the modern world. Said MSF advisor Dr. Susan Shepherd, "Children shouldn't have to deteriorate to the point of severe malnutrition to 'qualify' for ready-to-use food, which is far more nutritious than the fortified blended flours prescribed and supplied by the United States and other international donors for moderately malnourished children. Yes, ready-to-use food may cost more, but it provides the milk that

FIGURE 3.5 A 13-year-old Malawian boy stands back to back with a 12-year-old English boy in the village of Nyombe, located in the African country Malawi. The difference in height illustrates one of the effects of the difference in their nutrition.

fortified flours do not…. We need to focus on the food quality, not just the quantity." Today, it seems that only the financial efforts of wealthy countries can prevent the diseases of undernutrition.

REVIEW

Undernutrition is a kind of malnutrition caused by a deficit in calories, protein, or both. It is usually referred to as protein energy malnutrition (PEM). There are three main types of PEM: marasmus (generally a deficit in calories), kwashiorkor (generally protein deficiency), and marasmic kwashiorkor (a combination of the symptoms of both diseases). PEM can affect anyone of any age, but it is usually a disease striking young children in poor countries without an adequate food supply, perhaps due to war, famine, drought, or extreme poverty. It has severe, lifelong consequences and carries a high risk of mortality, even with proper treatment. Medical knowledge and means are available to both treat and prevent PEM, but it still affects an estimated 50 million children around the world. International food aid that concentrates on high-quality nutrition, protein, and easy distribution to every child in need is required to end hunger, malnutrition, and PEM.

OVERNUTRITION

For the first time in human history, more people are **overweight** than are hungry. About 1.6 billion people in the world are overweight or **obese**. Overnutrition is a condition in which the intake of calories (or energy) exceeds the use of calories. The extra energy is stored by the body as fat, and overweight and obesity are the result. Nutritionists call overnutrition an energy imbalance and consider it a true form of malnutrition. Overnutrition is not just about weighing too much; it is a real health danger that can cause serious disease and loss of life. In the United States alone, about 111,000 people die every year because of obesity-related illnesses.

OVERNUTRITION DISASTER

The problem of overnutrition is epidemic in many parts of the world today, and has proved difficult to treat or prevent. In the United States, nearly two of every three people are overweight. This includes about one-third of children and teens. The preva-

FIGURE 4.1 Overweight and obesity are forms of malnutrition called overnutrition and are serious health dangers. In overnutrition, the body's intake of calories, or energy, exceeds the use of calories, and the body stores the extra energy as fat. People with obesity—especially morbid obesity—are at a high risk for health problems and diseases such as diabetes, heart disease, and stroke.

lence of overweight in the United States is double what it was in 1960. Many other wealthy and rapidly developing countries are experiencing similar increases in the rates of overweight and obesity. The WHO considers this trend to be a global public health emergency. It explains that in some developing countries, overnutrition and undernutrition coexist. Also, in some developing countries, overnutrition rates are increasing faster than in wealthy countries. In a 2009 document titled "Obesity and Overweight," WHO officials wrote, "The health consequences range from increased risk of premature death to serious chronic conditions that reduce the overall quality of life. Of especial concern is the increasing incidence of child obesity." Some of the diseases that have been linked to chronic overweight and obesity include type 2 diabetes, high blood pressure, heart disease, and stroke.

DEFINING OVERNUTRITION: BMI

Overweight and obesity are defined medically as the accumulation of excess fat in the body. The percentage of excess fat compared to the estimated ideal body weight determines whether a person is overweight or obese. This amount is estimated using the body mass index (BMI), which is a mathematical formula and screening tool that compares height and weight. It is not an exact measure of excess fat, but, according to the U.S. Centers for Disease Control and Prevention (CDC), it is a simple and reliable estimate of "body fatness" for most adults. BMI is defined as weight in kilograms divided by height in meters squared ($BMI=kg/m^2$). The formula is converted to pounds and inches as weight divided by height squared, multiplied by 704.5 ($BMI=(lb/in^2)$ x 704.5). For example, a person who is 60 inches (1.5 meters) tall and weighs 112 pounds (50.8 kilograms) would have a BMI of 22. A BMI under 25 is considered a normal weight. If that same person weighed 133 pounds (60.3 kg), he or she would have a BMI of 26 and be considered overweight. Overweight is defined as a BMI between 25 and 29.9. If the person weighed 168 pounds (76 kg), he or she would have a BMI of 33 and test as obese. A BMI of 30 or more is considered obese. Many organizations, including the CDC, provide online BMI calculators.

BMI is a relatively accurate assessment of body weight in adults, but it is inaccurate for children and teens because they are still growing. In the case of young people under about age 20, a

BMI assessment must take into account age and gender, as well as height and weight. Healthy weight in young people can change from month to month as they grow, and it definitely changes from year to year. As an example, a boy with a BMI of 23 might be obese at age 10, but a healthy weight if he is 15.

BMI for children and teens is calculated as it is for adults, but then compared to percentile charts of average height and weight at different ages for boys and girls. A young person with a BMI at or above the 95th percentile is considered obese. This means his or her BMI is higher than 95% of all people of that sex and age. Young people with BMIs between the 85th and 95th percentiles

OBESE AND IN DANGER

When a person is 100 pounds (45.3 kg) or more over his or her ideal body weight, the condition is referred to as morbid obesity. This is a serious disease. Morbid obesity may also be defined as a BMI of 40 or greater, or as a BMI between 35 and 40 if accompanied by a serious medical problem, such as heart disease, diabetes, or joint pain. A BMI between 45 and 50 is severe morbid obesity. A BMI between 50 and 60 is super-morbid obesity. A BMI greater than 60 is super-super morbid obesity.

People with morbid obesity are at great risk of medical problems and disease if they do not lose weight. If they cannot reduce their weight by any other means, they are often eligible for bariatric surgery. This is weight-loss surgery in which the stomach and intestines are permanently modified.

Gastric bypass is one type of bariatric surgery. First, a small pouch is created at the top of the stomach by stapling it off from the rest of the stomach. Then the small intestine is cut so that its first section is no longer connected to the rest of the digestive system. The second section of the small intestine is sewn directly to the stomach pouch.

are overweight. Around the world, the WHO estimates that at least 22 million children under the age of 5 are overweight. In the United States, the number of overweight teens has tripled since 1980. Because overweight youth are likely to become overweight or obese adults, many nutritional and medical experts are particularly concerned about the health risks associated with childhood and teen overnutrition. These experts believe that early onset of obesity puts these young people at grave risk of disability and premature death in the future. In addition, many young people are developing obesity-related diseases that used to occur only in middle-aged or older adults.

The pouch is tiny—about the size of a walnut—and can hold only about 1 ounce (28 grams) of food. Calorie absorption also is limited by disconnecting, or bypassing, the first part of the small intestine. Many people experience drastic weight loss with gastric bypass surgery and vastly improve their health, but the risk of malnutrition is high. People take dietary supplements for life and learn a special diet that emphasizes proteins first.

Another bariatric procedure is called lap-band adjustable gastric banding. In this procedure, the doctor partitions the stomach into two parts with a flexible band or belt that creates only a tiny opening between the two parts of the stomach. This can make people feel full after very small meals. It is a simpler procedure than gastric bypass, but weight loss is not as extreme. In both cases, people who are not completely committed to the weight-loss program can overcome the procedures, gradually stretch their new stomachs, and regain weight. Neither procedure is a miracle cure for obesity, and people have to change their lifestyles permanently to achieve lasting good health and prevent disease.

METABOLIC SYNDROME

One of the major risk factors of overweight is the development of metabolic syndrome. Medical researchers estimate that at least 40 million people in the United States alone have metabolic syndrome. People with metabolic syndrome have at least three of the following disorders:

- They are overweight or obese, and fat is located mainly in the abdominal area.
- They have high blood pressure.
- The level of triglycerides (a form of fat) in their blood is too high.
- Bad cholesterol levels in the blood are high, and good cholesterol levels are too low.
- They have insulin resistance.

All of the disorders of metabolic syndrome are indications that the metabolism is overworked and not functioning well. No one knows with certainty what causes metabolic syndrome, but abdominal fat is strongly **correlated** with it. Scientists also know that a weight reduction can reduce or reverse these disorders.

Cholesterol and triglycerides are **lipids**, or fats, metabolized from foods and carried throughout the body in the bloodstream. Lipids are necessary for many organ functions, but when too much circulates in the blood, the vessels can become inflamed and clogged. This situation can increase the risk for arteriosclerosis—a narrowing and hardening of the blood vessels. If blood vessels become inflexible or are blocked by fatty deposits, heart disease and stroke can result, as blood flow is cut off to parts of the heart or brain. Reducing weight can reduce the lipids in the blood and significantly lower the risk of heart disease, stroke, and arteriosclerosis.

Insulin resistance can lead to severe physical damage, too. The pancreas makes insulin, the hormone that enables the body's cells

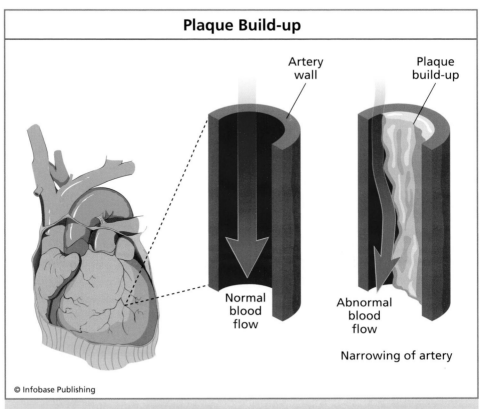

Plaque Build-up

Artery wall

Plaque build-up

Normal blood flow

Abnormal blood flow

Narrowing of artery

© Infobase Publishing

FIGURE 4.2 Plaque is made up of fat, cholesterol, calcium, and other substances. Plaque build-up can clog the arteries and increase the risk for arteriosclerosis, heart disease, and stroke.

to use glucose. Insulin can be thought of as the key that unlocks the cell and allows the glucose inside. Glucose cannot get into the cells without it. Under normal circumstances, when more glucose circulates in the blood, the pancreas makes more insulin. This allows glucose to enter cells, and lowers the glucose levels in the blood. When someone has insulin resistance, their cells don't respond to insulin as well. When glucose in the blood rises, the pancreas still makes insulin, but glucose doesn't go into cells as easily as it used to. The glucose levels in the blood remain high. As time passes, the overworked pancreas may begin to fail, as the cells that produce insulin begin to die. Type 2 diabetes is often the eventual outcome.

OVERWEIGHT AND TYPE 2 DIABETES

Type 2 diabetes is a serious disease. People with this disease have high levels of glucose in their blood. This is caused by the failure of the overworked pancreas to produce enough insulin, cells that are highly resistant to insulin, or both. Enough glucose is not getting inside cells, so the cells are damaged and malnourished. They can even "starve" to death if type 2 diabetes goes untreated. High blood glucose levels also are damaging to almost every organ in the body. Kidneys, which are overworked as they try to clean the excess glucose from the blood, can fail completely. Eyes are damaged and vision is lost. Nerve damage occurs, especially in the feet and legs. Sores and cuts are slow to heal. As people with diabetes lose feeling in their feet, they may be unaware of foot sores. Feet can become so damaged that they have to be amputated to save the person's life. People with type 2 diabetes also die of heart disease up to four times more often than people without diabetes.

Fortunately, type 2 diabetes is treatable. People with the disease strive to lose weight, eat carefully controlled diets, and usually take one or more medications to increase their insulin levels or decrease their insulin resistance. However, the struggle to control diabetes and avoid its complications is lifelong and not always successful. Most scientists believe that prevention is preferable to treatment, especially because type 2 diabetes has become a global epidemic and is affecting people at younger ages. Many experts believe that the obesity epidemic is the primary reason for the diabetes epidemic. However, most overweight people do not have diabetes, and not all people with diabetes are overweight. Finally, overweight and metabolic syndrome are difficult conditions to treat.

Medical science is not sure whether obesity leads to metabolic syndrome and diabetes, or whether metabolic syndrome and insulin resistance cause the propensity to be overweight. Scientists do know, however, that overweight and certain diseases occur together and that weight loss can reduce disease risk. If overweight people could achieve a healthy weight, millions of cases of diabetes, strokes, and heart disease likely would be prevented. Why is it so difficult to lose weight? Why do people become overweight in the first place? Today, researchers believe that the answers lie both in our lifestyles and in our genes.

GENES AND DNA

Genes are the packages of deoxyribonucleic acid (DNA) in the nuclei of almost every cell in the body. DNA carries the instructions for the development and functioning of every living thing. In humans, DNA is arranged in 23 pairs of chromosomes (one of each pair is inherited from each parent). Every chromosome is made up of genes. Genes are specific units of inheritance that code for a specific protein, so they determine how each cell operates. It is helpful to think of the chromosomes as recipes and the genes as the specific ingredients. DNA spells out the instructions for the ingredients. It writes the set of rules that tells each cell when and how to build its protein and do the work of the body.

Most DNA and genes are the same for everyone. Human genes make people into people, instead of plants or chimpanzees or mosquitoes. But some genetic instructions are different among people. This is why people look different from one another, have different talents and abilities, and are vulnerable to certain diseases. Changes in DNA and genes also occur when DNA is replicated. DNA is replicated, or copied, as a living thing develops from a single cell. It's also copied every day when cells divide to replace dying cells. These changes in DNA are like typographical errors. Some have no effect at all. Some can lead to disease. Some may cause slight differences in the way cells function. This is how evolution works. If the changes in DNA somehow increase the chances of that living thing surviving, the changes are more likely to get passed on to the next generation.

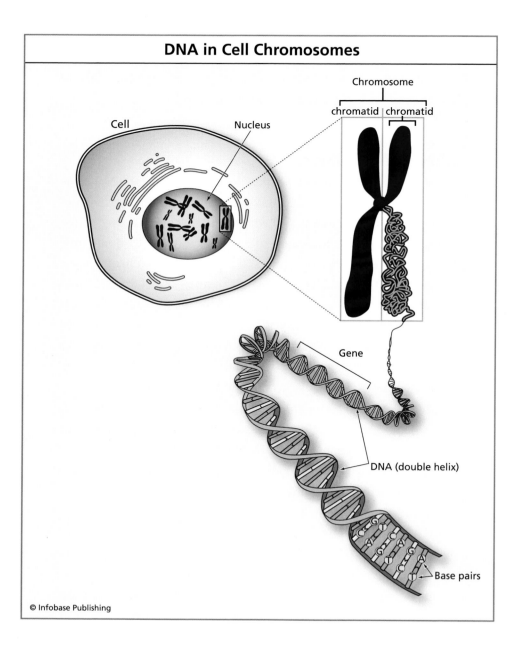

DNA in Cell Chromosomes

Chromosome

chromatid | chromatid

Cell

Nucleus

Gene

DNA (double helix)

Base pairs

THRIFTY GENES

Genetic differences in metabolism are one reason why some people gain weight easily and others stay thin. An efficient metabolism—making use of a large percentage of calories—would have helped our ancestors survive thousands, or even millions, of years ago.

Until quite recently in human history, people could not depend on a stable food supply. Historians believe that hunter-gatherers suffered regular, cyclical periods of feast or famine. People whose bodies easily stored extra nutrients as fat during the good times had the greatest chance of survival during the lean times. Bodies that hung on to extra calories the best were those with a very efficient metabolism that used glucose sparingly and stored the excess. Cells became insulin resistant so as to use as little glucose as possible. People with thrifty genes gained weight very easily, and, during the times of famine, their bodies resisted losing the excess fat. They metabolized it as slowly as possible, and were able to live off the stored nutrients until the famine was over. These people were evolutionary success stories. Instead of dying of starvation during times of famine, they survived and passed the thrifty genes on to their children.

This theory of the "thrifty gene" was proposed by James V. Neel in 1962 to explain the genetic determinants of obesity and insulin resistance. Today, scientists suspect that multiple genes are involved, and they have not yet identified them with certainty. Still, thrifty genes may account for at least part of the obesity epidemic of today.

We no longer live an arduous, feast-or-famine, hunter-gatherer lifestyle. We are inactive and consume a high-fat, high-sugar diet

(opposite page) **FIGURE 4.3** The long, stringy stand of DNA that makes up genes is spooled within chromosomes inside the nucleus of a cell. An actual gene would be a longer strand of DNA than is shown here.

that was completely unknown to our ancestors. Unfortunately, our genes do not "know" that things have changed. As a result, millions of people become overweight in preparation for the famine that never comes. Instead, they face diabetes, obesity, and chronic heart disease.

LIFESTYLES: THE OTHER HALF OF THE PROBLEM

Even if genes do play a major role in the development of overweight, no one is doomed by heredity to be obese or suffer the effects of overnutrition. Genes may make people vulnerable to overweight, but a person's lifestyle also has an effect. Nutritionists have identified several environmental factors that are probably responsible for the obesity epidemic of recent decades. In an article in the 2008 book *Nutrition in the Prevention and Treatment of Disease*, Nancy E. Sherwood and her research team identify the most important environmental determinants and risk factors in the development of obesity.

The researchers say that sedentary behavior and lack of physical activity seem to play a large role in overnutrition. Most sedentary behavior today is due to heavy amounts of screen time in adults and young people. "Screen time" refers to television, video games, computer use, and videos. Some studies suggest that screen time is taking the place of physical activity in the developed world. One report discovered that televisions, for example, are turned on more than seven hours a day in the average American household. In addition, many young people have few safe places to play or exercise. They have to be driven to organized activities. Parents may not have the time or money to invest in physically active hobbies for themselves or their children. The research team suggests that this problem, too, may lead to decreased activity. Sedentary pursuits ultimately mean less energy expenditure, more unused calories from foods, and increased weight gain.

ALTERED EATING HABITS

The quantity and types of foods consumed, however, may be the most important determinants of the obesity epidemic. Over the last few decades, eating patterns have changed in wealthy countries. Both the quantity of foods consumed and the energy density of the foods consumed have increased over the past 30 years. For example, in 1970, the average energy intake for adult men was 2,450 calories per day. By the year 2000, calorie intake had increased to 2,618. At the same time, consumption of energy-dense foods also increased. Energy density is the number of calories in a gram of food. (One gram equals about 0.035 ounces. A teaspoon of sugar weighs about 4.2 grams.) Fats, with 9 calories per gram, are much more energy dense than either carbohydrates or protein, at 4 calories per gram. High-fat diets are common in wealthy countries, often because of eating restaurant foods, prepackaged take-out meals, or fast foods. Fast-food meals, for example, are often 40% fat and very high in calories.

Snacks and sweets also contribute to high fat intake. Candy and potato chips, for instance, often have a high fat content. We have inherited tastes for sweet and fatty foods from our ancestors. The preference for sweet tastes, as opposed to bitter or sour ones, probably evolved as a defense against eating toxic plants or contaminated and spoiled foods, which often have a decidedly un-sweet taste. Humans came to crave sweet foods, and because they rarely found enough food to overeat, they were not harmed by their cravings. In a similar way, our bodies came to crave fatty foods because they were both rare and energy dense. Early humans needed to store as much energy as possible, and fats provided the most efficient energy storage. Sugars are quickly metabolized into glucose and energy. Fats and carbohydrates could mean the difference between survival and starvation. Now, even though fatty, sweet foods are plentiful, many people continue to prefer fat and sweet foods over many others.

Portion sizes have changed dramatically over the last few decades, and most people have accepted and learned to eat large portions of foods. In 1957, for instance, an average serving of soda was 8 ounces (0.2 liters). Today, it can be 64 ounces (1.9 L). A box of popcorn at the movies in 1957 held about 3 cups. Today, the average medium serving is 16 cups. An average muffin in 1957 weighed 1.5 ounces (42 g). Today it is 8 ounces (227 g). The same differences in portion sizes are found in meals and snack foods. A fast-food hamburger in the 1950s contained only about 1 ounce (28 g) of meat; a large hamburger served in a typical restaurant today may contain 6 ounces (170 g) of meat, and some super-sized hamburgers weigh more. One study found that, since 1977, everyone—both children and adults—increased portion sizes of all types of foods, whether eating out or at home.

Sherwood and her colleagues believe that several factors have contributed to the increases in portion sizes and intake of fatty, sweet foods. They cite television advertising for candy, snacks, sugary cereals, pizza, and fast foods. For children, they point to family eating practices, parental role modeling, and the decrease in the number of meals that families eat together. For both children and teens, the researchers advocate combating these trends with school-based educational programs about healthy nutrition and programs and opportunities for physical activity.

ADDICTED BRAINS

Dr. David Kessler, former commissioner of the U.S. Food and Drug Administration, agrees that advertising, the constant availability of foods, and cultural teaching contribute to overnutrition and the obesity epidemic. Still, he sees overnutrition as an addiction caused by modern exposure to foods rich in fats, salts, and sugars. In his 2009 book, *The End of Overeating: Taking Control of the Insatiable American Appetite*, he says that almost from infancy, people in wealthy countries are exposed to these foods. As a consequence, he explains, the pleasure centers of our brains are triggered and wired to crave more and more of them. Eventually, we are conditioned to need these foods in order to activate our pleasure centers—just as if these foods were addictive drugs or alcohol. He adds that foods that combine both sugar and fat, such as a milkshake or a candy bar, are the most addicting because of the powerful effects they have on the brain.

In a 2009 interview with Katharine Mieszkowski for the online magazine Salon.com, Kessler asserts that children are trained by age five to crave sweet and fatty foods. He says that we do not eat for nutrition. Instead, Kessler says, "We're eating for

OVERNOURISHED AND MALNOURISHED

During his lifetime, Michael Hebranko has been one of the heaviest people in the world. He admits that he is addicted to food. He has battled super morbid obesity for much of his life. When he was 15 years old, he already weighed 300 pounds (136 kg). He lost weight many times, only to regain it. In 1999, at age 34, he weighed 1,100 lbs (499 kg). After losing 700 pounds (317.5 kg), however, he went back to old habits. In 2007, he weighed about 600 pounds (272 kg) and entered a weight loss clinic. At that time, Hebranko was unable to walk and confined to his bed. He was also suffering severe bone pain that he feared was bone cancer. When doctors finally figured out a way to do a bone scan for Hebranko, they discovered that his problem was a vitamin deficiency disease. Hebranko had rickets or, as it is called in adults, osteomalacia. Because he stayed indoors all the time, he was never exposed to sunshine. Plus, his diet was unhealthy and did not include vitamin-enriched foods. Also, obese people do not absorb some vitamins as well as they would if they were a healthy weight. Hebranko was given high doses of vitamin D supplements, and in a few weeks was cured of the deficiency disease brought on by his extreme obesity. He began to walk again without pain. By 2009, at age 55, Hebranko was doing well with his weight loss and health and had dropped to about 350 lbs (159 kg).

FIGURE 4.4 Portion sizes have increased over the past few decades, and people are eating larger portions than what is considered a serving. For instance, a portion of pasta the size of a tennis ball is considered one serving.

stimulation." Brain addiction is why weight-loss diets fail, and people quickly regain the pounds they have lost. It is why people do not experience feeling full and cannot resist their favorite foods. Their brains are constantly rewarded for overeating. They are continually anticipating the pleasure of food because they are surrounded by cues that tell them to eat. Eventually, just the sight of a favorite food is enough to trigger the demand to eat it, even when we are not hungry. Kessler says our brains have been hijacked. He believes the answer to this dilemma is "food rehab," and teaching oneself new food rules so as to rewire the brain. Old learning cannot be erased altogether, but new learning can help people get over the addiction.

Kessler was once overweight, and he knows how difficult retraining the brain can be. He also recognizes that no one knows the best approach, but he thinks understanding the addiction is the first step. Then, he says, people can give their brains new messages about food. He suggests, for instance, "If you look at a huge plate of fries and say 'That's my friend, that's going to make me feel better, I want that,' that's only going to increase the level of anticipation. You look at that huge plate of fries and say, 'That's not my friend, that's going to make me feel pretty crummy in 20 minutes. I don't want that,' and you internalize that, then you can decrease the anticipation."

NUTRITIONAL EDUCATION

Psychologist and obesity researcher Eric Stice of the Oregon Research Institute believes that prevention of obesity depends on giving young people nutritional messages and education that permanently affect their lifestyles. Stice is particularly interested in preventing obesity and other eating disorders in teens. In 2005, Stice and his research team enrolled a group of college-aged women in a four-week healthy eating class. They learned how to reduce fats and sugars in their diets and the importance of increasing physical activity. They kept food and exercise diaries.

In class sessions, they discussed maintaining a healthy energy balance. Three years later, Stice contacted and evaluated the young women. He discovered a 55% decrease in the number of cases of overweight as compared to young women who were not enrolled in the classes. For the first time, science had evidence that intervention programs can help young people maintain a healthy weight.

As a result of his studies, Stice developed a program called Healthy Weight, which is an educational, healthy lifestyle intervention for teens. Stice's institute trains teachers and counselors to offer the program in high schools and colleges around the country. The sessions emphasize moderation and healthy eating, not weight-loss diets. Stice and many other researchers believe such diets are of little value and can actually trigger overeating and eventual obesity. Participants in Healthy Weight sessions are taught nutrition facts and encouraged to make simple changes in their lives. They are asked to gradually reduce the least healthy foods they eat (one at a time) and gradually increase healthy foods—the ones their ancestors ate, such as lean proteins, whole grains, fruits, and vegetables. The teens also gradually add exercise to their daily routine. These lifestyle changes are meant to be permanent, so slow and easy is the best approach. Stice says that no one is ever pushed to conform to a specific program. No calorie counting or exercise rules are taught. Instead, participants make their own decisions about how to improve their lifestyles, and, according to Stice, follow-up studies indicate that this approach works quite well in developing healthy attitudes and preventing obesity.

Despite his success with lifestyle interventions, Stice is well aware that the determinants of obesity involve genes and brain wiring, as well as habits and attitudes. In brain-imaging studies comparing the brains of obese people to lean people, Stice has identified differences in reactivity in certain parts of the brain. In the studies, he found that the parts of the brain responsible for taste and bodily sensation are more active in obese people fed rich milkshakes than in lean people fed the same milkshakes. At the same time, the brain region that controls feeling rewarded by food is less active in obese people than it is in lean people. These results may explain why some people crave certain foods more than others do and why they need more of that food to feel satisfied.

NO EASY ANSWERS

Currently, Stice and his team are searching for the genetic variations that could account for these brain differences. They do not know whether the brain differences are genetic or created by the long-term intake of high-fat, high-sugar foods, or whether both play a role. Stice and other scientists hope to identify the causes of these variations and to find ways to predict who is vulnerable to obesity long before it occurs. If this were possible, either medical or lifestyle interventions might prevent obesity altogether. For now, however, the search for effective obesity prevention programs continues, and obesity continues to be a devastating, intractable problem for millions of people. Researchers may not completely understand all the causes of obesity or how best to prevent it, but they do know that high-fat, high-sugar diets are unhealthy, not only because of the diseases associated with obesity, but also because the nutritional value of such diets is far from ideal.

REVIEW

Overnutrition is a form of malnutrition in which the intake of calories exceeds the amount of calories expended. As a result of this energy imbalance, excess calories are stored as fat, and the individual becomes overweight or obese. Overweight is measured by Body Mass Index (BMI). In adults, a BMI under 25 is defined as a healthy weight. A BMI between 25 and 29 is defined as overweight. A BMI equal to or more than 30 defines obesity. Overweight and obesity are associated with the development of chronic diseases such as metabolic syndrome, type 2 diabetes, heart disease, and stroke. Around the world, the incidence of obesity has increased dramatically during the last few decades and is having disastrous public health consequences. Researchers blame both genetics and lifestyles for the obesity epidemic. Unlike their ancestors, modern people are eating high-fat, high-sugar diets with increased portion sizes. At the same time, they are becoming increasingly sedentary. Thousands of years of evolution have resulted in efficient human metabolisms that store and maintain excess fat in preparation for famine. Brains become addicted to high-fat, high-sugar foods, and this makes it difficult to choose healthy foods. Researchers suggest that nutritional education to help young people make healthier lifestyle choices and re-training the brain to reject unhealthy foods are the best options available to combat the obesity epidemic.

MICRONUTRIENT INSUFFICIENCY

The diets of people in wealthy countries may include too many calories and the wrong balance of macronutrients, but these same diets are often insufficient in micronutrients. This does not mean that people get micronutrient deficiency diseases such as goiter or rickets, but it does mean that their diets are deficient enough to prevent optimum health. Nutritionists and medical doctors refer to this condition as suboptimal or insufficient micronutrient intake. No one is completely sure how much of each micronutrient is ideal. But many experts believe that millions of people are overfed but undernourished. The more researchers learn about nutrition, the more they suspect that micronutrients in the correct quantities are essential protection against many diseases.

RECOMMENDED DIETARY ALLOWANCES

The Food and Nutrition Board of the U.S. National Academy of Sciences periodically provides updated recommendations for nutrient intakes for people in the United States and Canada. These recommendations are called Dietary Reference Intakes (DRI). They are standards for energy (calories), 14 vitamins, 15 minerals, and 7 macronutrients. Current recommendations do not focus only on the micronutrient intakes necessary to prevent deficiency diseases. They also focus on nutritional requirements to reduce the risk of chronic disease, and the amount of each nutrient necessary for optimal health. The task is complex because nutritional requirements vary from person to person. They depend on activity level, age, habits, and health status, as well as genetics and the environment in which a person lives. Therefore, recommendations are usually made so they will benefit the majority of the population.

Based on previous scientific studies, the Food and Nutrition Board attempts to establish an "estimated average requirement" (EAR). This is the intake that would be enough to maintain good health and reduce disease risk for about half the population. A recommended dietary allowance (RDA) is established based upon the EAR. An RDA is mathematically figured by adding two standard deviations to the EAR so that the recommended amount of the nutrient would be adequate for about 97.5% of the population. In instances where there is not enough scientific data to set RDAs, the Food and Nutrition Board sets a best estimate for the nutrient, called "adequate intake" (AI).

For the vast majority of people, according to the Food and Nutrition Board, following the RDAs for each nutrient should support optimum health. However, because men and women have different nutritional needs, RDAs are established separately by gender. Children and teens need different standards, too, because they are growing. The ideal micronutrient intake for any individual is almost never known, but the RDA standards are the best guidelines available. They offer the best chance of lowering disease risk and avoiding micronutrient insufficiency.

In the United States, the vast majority of normal people easily meet the standards for calories and most macronutrients,

TABLE 5.1 ADEQUACY OF SELECTED MICRONUTRIENTS IN THE DIETS OF U.S. ADULTS (AGES 19 TO 50) AS COMPARED WITH RDAS OR AIS

Micronutrient	Gender	Recommended Daily Intake (RDA or AI)	Percent that does not meet this intake
Vitamin A	Men	900 mcg (micrograms)	57%
	Women	700 mcg	48%
Vitamin C	Men	90 mg (milligrams)	36%
	Women	75 mg	32%
Vitamin E	Men	15 mg	89%
	Women	15 mg	97%
Vitamin B6	Men	1.3 mg–1.7 mg	7%
	Women	1.3 mg–1.5 mg	28%
Folate (folic acid)	Men	400 mcg	6%
	Women	400 mcg	16%
Vitamin B12	Men	2.4 mcg	<3%
	Women	2.4 mcg	7%–9%
Iron	Men	8 mg	< 3%
	Women	8 mg–18 mg	10%
Zinc	Men	11 mg	11%
	Women	8 mg	17%
Magnesium	Men	400 mg–420 mg	64%
	Women	310 mg–320 mg	67%

Based on the U.S. Centers for Disease Control and Prevention's National Health and Nutrition Examination Survey, 2001-2002.

but many diets are inadequate in micronutrients, especially if foods alone are considered, without the addition of vitamin and mineral supplements. Some micronutrients, such as B12, B6, and iron are maintained at healthy levels by most adults, but other nutrients, such as vitamin E, vitamin A, and magnesium are not. The National Health and Nutrition Examination Survey, done by the U.S. Centers for Disease Control and Prevention, reports that many Americans eat diets that don't contain enough of one or more nutrients. In general, the report says, young children eat more nutritious diets than teens or adults, although children are often deficient in vitamin E. Magnesium intake is especially low among female teens—98% of them do not get enough magnesium. Teen girls are also reported to have an inadequate intake of zinc. Calcium and folate (a B vitamin) are inadequate in both teens and adults, according to RDA standards. For all people, those living in poverty eat less nutritious diets than those with high standards of living. Those who are overweight also are more likely to eat less nutritious diets than people of healthy weight.

Some nutritional studies suggest that as many as 75% of people in the United States do not meet RDA requirements for one or more micronutrients. Yet, many nutritional researchers argue that RDAs are set too low for optimum health. It's not clear how suboptimal levels of micronutrients harm the body, because many micronutrients have multiple functions. As research continues, more health risks are linked with nutritional inadequacy and an imbalance of vitamins and minerals.

VITAMIN C AND THE IMMUNE SYSTEM

A person who does not get enough vitamin C may not develop a deficiency disease, but his or her immune system does not function as well as it could. Vitamin C apparently helps to maintain good levels of antibodies to fight off infections. At least three kinds of antibodies appear to be strengthened by adequate vitamin C. They are IgA, IgM, and IgG. IgA is the immunoglobulin found

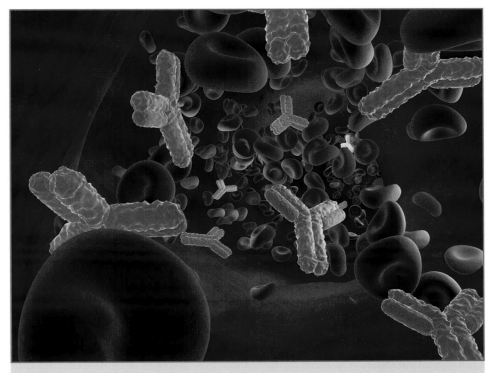

FIGURE 5.1 Vitamin C appears to help maintain good levels of antibodies within the blood to fight off infections.

in mucous membranes. IgM is the immunoglobulin that activates other parts of the immune system when a foreign invader is detected. IgG is the immunoglobulin circulating in the blood that fights viruses. It also is passed through the blood to a developing fetus and gives the baby some antibody protection from birth.

In one study, in South Africa, a group of people were given vitamin C supplements daily for about three months. When their blood was tested at the end of the experiment, researchers discovered 20% higher IgM levels compared with a second group that received no extra vitamin C. IgG levels rose slightly in the people receiving vitamin C, too. IgA levels stayed the same in the group that took supplements, but in the other group, IgA levels dropped 15%. The researchers noted that IgA levels normally drop in the winter (when this study was conducted). No one knows why this should occur, but the study showed that the drop could be prevented with added vitamin C.

OTHER MICRONUTRIENT ESSENTIALS

Vitamin C is not the only micronutrient that benefits the immune system. Several vitamins and minerals seem to be essential for optimal immune system functioning. Vitamin A is particularly important because it helps make the white blood cells called lymphocytes. There are several types of white blood cells involved in fighting infections. Lymphocytes circulate in the lymph nodes, thymus gland, and spleen. They identify foreign invaders and then produce antibodies. Vitamin B6 plays a critical role in the functioning of the spleen, thymus gland, and lymph nodes. Without enough vitamin B6, the number of lymphocytes and antibodies in these organs is reduced.

Vitamin D increases the immune system's production of peptides, which are chains of amino acids that are smaller than protein amino acid chains and that can destroy viruses. Vitamin D also helps to prevent inflammation and helps stop the immune system from destroying the body's own cells. The immune system normally recognizes foreign proteins while leaving the body's own proteins alone. When this system fails, the body may attack itself, causing **autoimmune diseases**. Vitamin D helps the recognition system to function correctly.

Minerals are involved in immune system functioning, too. Zinc is especially important. It plays a role in the production and activation of T cells, which are lymphocytes. It also helps build the other major white blood cells, called neutrophils. They are produced in the bone marrow, in the centers of bones. Neutrophils circulate in the bloodstream. They react to any bacterial infection, move to the infected tissue, and fight the infection. Neutrophils multiply dramatically when a bacterial infection is detected. The greater the infection, the more of these white blood cells are produced. Zinc helps neutrophils multiply. Like all blood cells, each neutrophil has a short life, so the bone marrow must continually replace dying cells with new ones. Zinc is necessary for this function.

Cells must continually be replaced in the skin, as well. So zinc is related to skin health, too. Zinc not only boosts the immune system's ability to prevent acne, rashes, boils, and other skin diseases, but also helps to transport vitamin A to the skin. Without adequate zinc, cells cannot metabolize vitamin A efficiently. Vitamin A is required by many organ systems in the body, and it is also effective in preventing or healing acne.

THE ANTIOXIDANTS

Vitamins A, C, and E, as well as the trace mineral selenium, are important **antioxidants** that protect cell health and may play critical roles in cancer prevention. Antioxidant vitamins and minerals are micronutrients that can prevent and often heal cell damage. When cells metabolize nutrients and build their proteins, chemical processes take place that can lead to the release of **free radicals**. Free radicals are unstable atoms that tend to form when oxygen interacts with cell molecules. This interaction is called oxidation. The free radicals released during oxidation and normal cell functioning then react with other atoms in other cells. These interactions can create a domino effect, causing reactions in large numbers of cells.

DNA in the cells can be damaged because of free radicals. Cell membranes (which are the outer "skin" of cells and keep them intact) can be damaged or destroyed. Cells may function poorly or die from the damage that free radicals can do. Scientists believe that free radicals are ultimately responsible for the aging process, for causing some tissue damage, and for many diseases, such as cancers. As a real-life example of oxidation, the American Dietetic Association suggests thinking about what happens when you slice an apple in half. As the white flesh is exposed to the oxy-

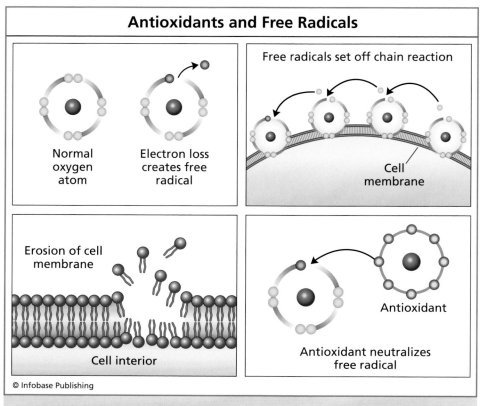

Antioxidants and Free Radicals

Normal oxygen atom

Electron loss creates free radical

Free radicals set off chain reaction

Cell membrane

Erosion of cell membrane

Cell interior

Antioxidant

Antioxidant neutralizes free radical

© Infobase Publishing

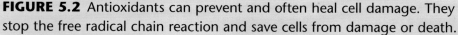

FIGURE 5.2 Antioxidants can prevent and often heal cell damage. They stop the free radical chain reaction and save cells from damage or death.

gen in the air, it begins to turn brown. That is oxidation. However, plunge the apple into orange juice and the oxidation stops. The vitamin C in the orange juice is the antioxidant that counteracts the browning process.

Antioxidants protect cells in the body in a similar way. They are the body's defense system that stops the free radical chain reaction and saves cells from damage or death. Antioxidant enzymes seek out or "scavenge" free radicals, but these enzymes cannot function without antioxidant vitamins and minerals. Our bodies need to maintain a balance between oxidants and antioxidants. Normal cell functioning leads to the release of free radicals, but so do environmental stresses such as cigarette smoking, pollutants, x-rays, and radiation from the sun. This is why a regular intake of antioxidant micronutrients is necessary for the maintenance of cell health. Without enough antioxidants, the body comes under oxidative stress.

Free radicals damage all the substances in a cell, including proteins, lipids, and carbohydrates. Destroyed proteins may lead to cataracts in the eyes. Free radicals' effects on essential lipids may lead to heart disease. Free radical damage accumulating in cells over time may be why people progressively develop the symptoms and diseases of old age. When DNA is damaged by free radicals, the genetic instructions can be changed. If DNA damage in a cell is too great to be repaired, one of three things happens to the cell: It can go into a kind of sleep state called senescence (old age); it may "commit suicide," which is known as **apoptosis** or programmed cell death; or it may start dividing or replicating in an uncontrolled way. Uncontrolled cell growth can lead to cancer.

CAN ANTIOXIDANTS HEAL CANCER?

Exactly how cancer develops is not yet completely known, but a lack of antioxidants probably plays a role. Several studies have shown that people who eat diets high in fruits and vegetables (in which most antioxidants are found) are less likely to be diagnosed with cancer and heart disease. When scientists try to test this association with high doses of particular antioxidants, however, there are mixed results. Some experiments have shown that extra doses of vitamins A and E have reduced cases of colon cancer and **gastrointestinal** cancers in groups of people. One study of selenium—the Nutritional Prevention of Cancer Trial—concluded that overall cancers were reduced by 37% in people who received this mineral supplement long term.

However, several studies have found that extra vitamin and mineral supplements do not protect people from cancer. Several studies have even found increased lung cancer rates in smokers who took high doses of vitamin A. Writing in *Nutrition in the Prevention and Treatment of Disease*, Harold E. Seifried and John A. Milner suggest that this may reflect a difference in nutritional status. They say that people who already have enough antioxidant nutrients from foods might not be helped by supplements. Yet, people who do not have enough antioxidants are protected by supplements. Scientists believe that vitamin A is metabolized differently in smokers than in nonsmokers. In addition, oxidants and antioxidants have to be in balance for metabolism to function correctly. Sometimes, for instance, preventing cell death is not desirable. Antioxidants in smokers may actually protect cancer cells, allowing them to multiply, instead of allowing the immune system to attack and kill them.

ANTIOXIDANT TOP 20

In 2004, scientists with the United States Department of Agriculture measured the antioxidant levels of more than 100 foods. The top 20 foods for prevention of free radical damage, in descending order of antioxidant levels, are:

20. Pecans
19. Mexican red beans
18. Red kidney beans
17. Walnuts
16. Pinto beans
15. Hazelnuts
14. Cranberries
13. Artichoke hearts
12. Wild blueberries
11. Prunes

10. Black beans
9. Pistachio nuts
8. Black plums
7. Blackberries
6. Raspberries
5. Almonds
4. Black-eyed peas
3. Red Delicious apples
2. Granny Smith apples
1. Dates

Another problem with studies of antioxidants is that researchers still do not know how micronutrients interact with each other and within the body. Many micronutrients from supplements are not absorbed as well as the same micronutrients ingested naturally from foods, yet at other times, the reverse is true. Also, scientists do not know how to measure oxidative stress. They are not sure how medicines interact with micronutrients. And they are not certain how much of each micronutrient is ideal for the prevention or treatment of diseases, such as cancer.

Laboratory tests in petri dishes show that antioxidants keep tumor cells from growing. Many studies have shown that people who eat foods rich in antioxidants are healthier than people who do not. But people who eat a balanced diet that includes lots of fruits and vegetables are ingesting many more micronutrients than antioxidants. They are probably getting other substances that have not yet been identified as essential to health. That is why the American Heart Association does not recommend antioxidant supplements. Instead, the Association says that people should get their micronutrients from eating a wide variety of antioxidant-rich fruits, vegetables, whole grains, and nuts.

FOOD CHOICES AND INSUFFICIENCIES

Whether for antioxidants or other micronutrients, the goal for everyone should be a varied diet that avoids nutritional insufficiencies and protects health. In wealthy countries, too many people fail at this goal. They choose foods with little or no nutritional value and lots of calories. Examples of these foods are soda, candy, snack foods, and processed foods. Processed foods—such as white flour, white rice, convenience foods, sugary cereals, and high-fat foods—are changed from their natural state to make them tastier or more appealing, or to preserve them. Not all processed foods are bad, but when nutrients are stripped away, the foods are no longer healthy in all the ways that our bodies need. Most processed foods have been enriched or fortified, so that some, but not all of the missing nutrients are replaced. Yet, enrichment of foods cannot prevent all the micronutrient insufficiencies in modern diets, because people continue to make food choices that omit fruits and vegetables, substitute soda for milk, or replace fish and lean meat with cheeseburgers and bologna.

THE MIRACLE OF FOLIC ACID

Even a well-understood micronutrient can have a surprising, unsuspected role to play in the prevention of disease. In 1991, for example, Dr. Nicholas Wald conducted an experiment with pregnant English women who already had one child with a neural tube defect. Neural tube defects are birth defects in which early fetal development of the brain and spinal cord goes awry. The most common neural tube defects are spina bifida and anencephaly. In spina bifida, the child is born with an opening somewhere along the spinal cord. The birth defect can cause multiple problems, including paralysis, hydrocephalus (increased fluid pressure in the brain), and incontinence (inability to control bowel and urinary functions). Children with anencephaly are missing most of their brains. These terrible birth defects affect approximately 500,000 children each year, and sometimes run in families.

Dr. Wald wanted to know whether supplementing a pregnant woman's diet with folic acid—a B vitamin, also known as folate—could help reduce the incidence of neural tube defects. His experiment was based on reports from medical doctors that pregnant patients with a kind of anemia caused by a folic acid deficiency would sometimes give birth to children with anencephaly or spina bifida. Half of the mothers in Wald's experiment were given 4 micrograms (mcg) of folic acid daily. (A microgram is one one-thousandth of a milligram or one one-millionth of a gram.) The other half were not. Wald had planned a long-term experiment, but the results were so dramatic that he stopped the study prematurely. In the mothers receiving folic acid supplements, he had reduced the incidence of spina bifida and anencephaly by 72%. Startlingly, the answer to a serious and mysterious birth defect that had occupied the attention of researchers for years was a simple vitamin supplement.

Today, the incidence of spina bifida in the United Kingdom is 95% lower than it was in 1991, and, in 2008, Dr. Wald was knighted by the Queen for his work with folic acid and neural tube defects. Newly pregnant women are routinely given folic acid supplements by their physicians. Around the world, medical doctors hailed Wald's discovery. In the United States, Dr. Godfrey Oakley called the news of Wald's experiment the most wonderful and important in his career. Oakley was the director of the division on birth defects for the U.S. Centers for Disease Control and Prevention. He began a campaign to have folic acid added to flour, rice, and pasta

FOLIC ACID: A WEDDING STORY

Dr. Godfrey Oakley is on a mission, and his dream is a world without birth defects. He is determined to spread the word about using folic acid to prevent spina bifida and anencephaly. Whenever he and his wife are invited to a wedding, their gift is a year's supply of folic acid supplements for the bride. Sometimes, when he is invited to a wedding reception, he shows up with a briefcase stuffed with folic acid supplements for all the women there. When he was interviewed on PBS's News Hour, he brought extra folic acid supplements to give to the program's staff. Dr. Oakley always explains why he is giving his rather unusual presents. He explains that neural tube defects begin early in fetal development, before most women know they are pregnant. Taking supplements after a pregnancy is confirmed may be too late to prevent birth defects. Therefore, folic acid supplements should be taken by all women of childbearing age—just in case. He invites people to gift every bride with folic acid.

in the United States. That campaign succeeded in 1998. Oakley continues to urge folic acid fortification of staple foods in countries around the world. He believes that spina bifida continues to occur in wealthy countries only because not enough folic acid is added to staple foods. He wants the current amount increased, and he says that it should be added to cornmeal as well.

THE LIFE YOU SAVE COULD BE YOUR OWN

Folic acid was identified as an essential vitamin decades before Wald's discovery. Scientists knew it was important for the functioning of DNA. But no one knew that inadequate folic acid was the cause of a severe and common birth defect. Wald's breakthrough leads us to wonder what other diseases might be prevented with optimal nutrition. It is strong evidence that everyone should care about eating a diet that is rich in micronutrients. (Dr. Oakley notes that spinach is an excellent source of folic acid.)

REVIEW

Not getting enough micronutrients is a kind of undernourishment. Disease sometimes results. Even if micronutrient insufficiency is not severe enough to cause disease, it can put stress on the body's organs and systems. It also can play a major role in ill health, cancers, and even birth defects. The U.S. National Academy of Sciences puts out guidelines about how much of each micronutrient people should get each day. These are called Recommended Dietary Allowances (RDAs). The majority of people in the United States and other wealthy countries eat diets that do not meet RDAs for one or more micronutrients. The immune system's healthy functioning depends on the proper balance of several micronutrients. Insufficiencies of these vitamins and minerals can lead to increased infections, poor healing, and a failure of the signaling system that identifies foreign invaders. Antioxidant micronutrients are suspected to be of critical importance to maintaining cell health and the prevention of cancers. A diet that includes foods rich in antioxidants seems to dramatically reduce the risk of cancer. Researchers do not yet know all the ways that an insufficiency of micronutrients can harm the body, but they believe that many modern diseases may be caused, at least in part, by not getting enough vitamins and minerals. Adequate folic acid, for instance, was recently discovered to be critical to the prevention of the serious birth defects spina bifida and anencephaly. What other diseases might be prevented by optimal micronutrient intake? No one knows the answer to this question, so the safest approach is to eat a varied diet that includes all micronutrients in abundance.

NUTRITION AND PROBLEMS OF METABOLISM

Some people are born with genetic variations or errors that mean one or more of the nutrients in foods cannot be absorbed, utilized, or turned into energy. These conditions used to be disabling or deadly; today, many of them are treatable, even when the disorder itself cannot be altered or cured. Specialized nutrition therapy can prevent disability and further diseases that used to result from these disorders.

INBORN ERRORS OF METABOLISM

Inborn errors of metabolism (IEMs) also are called congenital metabolic diseases. They usually are obvious from birth, but sometimes are not diagnosed until childhood or adulthood. Each specific IEM is rare, but there are hundreds of them, so the overall incidence of metabolic disorders is common. An IEM occurs in about 1 in every 5,000 births. IEMs usually are caused by a defect in a single gene, which codes for a particular enzyme. Enzymes do all the work inside cells. They are required to change a **substrate** (the nutrient being broken down) into the product (another new substance that is needed by the body). For example, the enzyme lactase breaks down lactose, the sugar in milk. If a person is missing lactase or does not produce enough, milk cannot be digested and metabolized, so the person is lactose intolerant.

When there is not enough of an enzyme, the substrate builds up, and the product is found at very low levels, or not at all. The result may be uncomfortable and painful, as in lactose intolerance, or it may be life threatening. Toxic substances may build up in the body. Cells may no longer function normally and have a reduced ability to make their own compounds or produce energy from the foods that are eaten. IEMs can be disorders of protein metabolism, fat metabolism, or carbohydrate metabolism, depending on the specific enzyme affected. The enzyme is malfunctioning or missing because the gene that codes for it is missing or defective.

GENES AND IEMS

In metabolic disorders, genetic dysfunction is usually inherited. When a human egg is fertilized, the resulting **zygote** inherits 23 chromosomes from its mother and 23 from its father. The chromosomes that determine sex are the X and Y chromosomes. A male zygote has inherited a Y from the father and an X from the mother (XY). A female inherited an X from each parent (XX). X chromosomes carry many genes that determine traits other than gender. Y chromosomes carry very few genes. The other 22 pairs of chromosomes are called autosomal, meaning they are not sex-linked. They carry genes for thousands of traits and body functions, and these genes, too, are inherited by the zygote in pairs—one from each parent. In many cases, the genes in the pair can be dominant or recessive. A simple way to understand dominant and recessive genes is with eye color. If a developing fetus has inherited an **allele** (form of a gene) for brown eyes from its father and an allele for blue eyes from its mother, the infant will

GOT MILK? NO THANKS!

Infant mammals depend on their mothers' milk. Thus, almost all mammals, including humans, are born with the ability to make large amounts of the enzyme lactase. Lactose, the sugar in milk, is metabolized by lactase. Once childhood is over, most mammals do not make as much of this enzyme, or stop making it altogether. Humans are the exception; some continue to make lactase throughout adulthood. Yet, most humans do not. Scientists estimate that 60% to 75% of the world's population does not make lactase as adults. As a result, they are lactose intolerant. Almost all Asians and Native Americans, and about 75% of African Americans are lactose intolerant. But about 90% of Northern Europeans and small percentages of Africans and Middle Easterners continue to make lactase. They have gene mutations that allow lactase production to continue. This may have been a survival mechanism. Scientists believe the mutation occurred about 10,000 years ago. At that time, humans in Northern Europe began dairy farming and raising domesticated animals. In winter, when stored crops and meats ran low, the lactose-tolerant people could depend on milk from their tame animals to help them survive. Many modern people of European ancestry retain this gene mutation. Thirteen separate groups of people in Africa and the Middle East retain lactose tolerance, too, although it is due to different genes than the European gene. The ancestors of these people were nomadic and regularly migrated with their domesticated cattle, seeking pasture for the animals to eat and depending on the milk from their cattle to survive. Modern descendants of these nomads retain the ability to metabolize lactose. The rest of the world suffers from trying to digest milk. They have symptoms that include bloating, gas, nausea, diarrhea, and stomach pain. Lactose intolerance, however, is not really a disease. It is the normal situation for most mammalian adults, human or otherwise.

be born with brown eyes. Brown is dominant. The infant carries one blue-eyed gene, but the gene is not expressed. It is recessive. It is still there and still can be passed on to future generations, but only a baby who inherits two alleles for blue eyes—one from each parent—will actually have blue eyes. Because that infant has no allele for brown eyes, he or she cannot pass on the dominant brown-eyed trait.

Many inborn errors of metabolism are inherited in the same way that eye color is inherited. Each parent had one normal, dominant gene that coded for an enzyme and one recessive, defective gene that did not. The parents, because of their dominant healthy genes, had no metabolic disorder, but they were both carriers for the disorder. An offspring of these parents may receive both defective genes. Such an infant is said to have inherited an autosomal recessive disorder. Each baby born to these parents has a 25% chance of being healthy (inheriting two normal genes); a 50% chance of being healthy, but a carrier for the disease (inheriting one normal and one defective gene); and a 25% chance of inheriting the inborn error of metabolism.

Not all IEMs are inherited in this way. Some are the result of faulty genes on the X chromosome, and some happen because of mutations that can occur when DNA is replicating itself and cells are dividing as a zygote grows into a fetus. However, many of the most common IEMs are autosomal recessive disorders.

PKU

PKU (phenylketonuria) is an autosomal recessive disorder in which the enzyme called phenylalanine hydroxylase is missing because the gene that codes for the enzyme is defective. An infant born missing this enzyme cannot break down an amino acid called phenylalanine (the substrate) into the amino acid tyrosine (the product). Tyrosine is used as a building block in the nervous system and brain. Toxic levels of phenylalanine begin to build up in the body immediately. If it is not recognized and treated, PKU leads to brain damage, severe mental retardation, hyperactivity, and seizures.

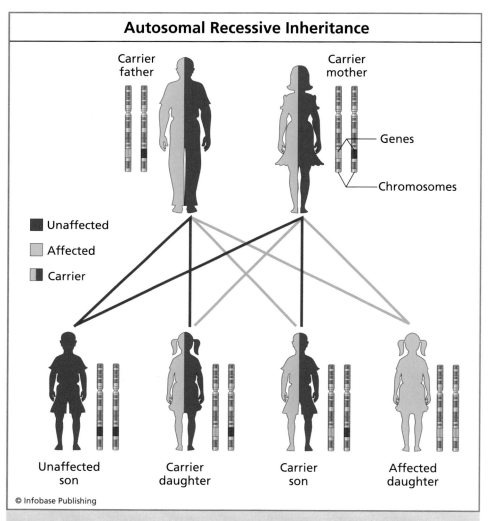

FIGURE 6.1 In autosomal recessive inheritance, a person has the condition if he or she has two copies of the gene—usually one from the mother and one from the father. A carrier has only one copy of the gene and does not have the condition, but he or she carries the gene and will be more likely to have children with the condition.

In the past, children with PKU were hopelessly retarded and usually ended up in institutions. Today, however, U.S. state laws and regulations in many other countries require that hospitals screen every newborn for PKU, as well as other metabolic disorders. Babies who test positive for PKU are immediately placed on special diets. This nutritional therapy is a method of "working around" the missing enzyme by using a diet that does not include phenylalanine. These diets are not easy to formulate or tolerate, however. Phenylalanine is in bread, cake, crackers, meat, eggs, fish, nuts, and dairy products. Protein is a requirement for healthy growth and body maintenance, but people with PKU must eat a very low-protein diet. Babies with PKU are fed artificial formulas made up of other amino acids, and the formula is bitter and distasteful. Throughout their lives, people with PKU have to drink these amino acid supplements to get the protein they need. Most people are allowed some fruits and vegetables, some breads, and a very small amount of dairy products. Tyrosine supplements have been developed, and these are given to people with PKU in an effort to replace the missing tyrosine that the body is unable to make. Vitamin and mineral supplements are also needed because of the very restricted diet. The diet is boring and difficult, but people who follow it have normal intelligence and lead normal, healthy lives. PKU cannot be cured, but dietary intervention is a true success story.

MAPLE SUGAR URINE DISEASE

Maple sugar urine disease is another autosomal recessive disorder of protein metabolism. It is named for the sweet smell of the urine of affected people. In this disease, the enzymes for breaking down leucine, isoleucine, and valine are defective. These amino acids build up in the blood. Maple sugar urine disease may be mild or severe, depending on how the enzymes function and the blood levels of the amino acids. In its most severe form, the disease can lead to loss of appetite, vomiting, mental retardation, seizures, and

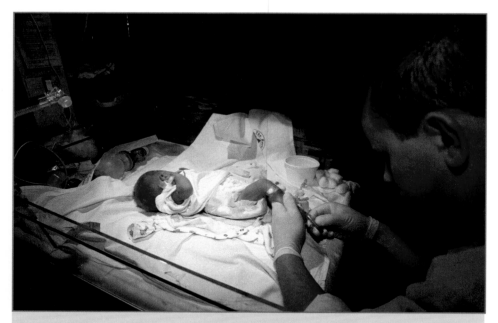

FIGURE 6.2 Laws in the United States and many other countries require that all newborns be tested for PKU. Although there is no cure, immediate dietary intervention can help these babies grow up to lead normal, healthy lives. Here, a premature infant in high dependency intensive care gets a blood sample taken.

coma. Untreated infants die within the first few months of life. Even people with mild forms of maple sugar urine disease may die if their bodies are under stress from infection and their disorder is untreated. As with PKU, treatment is nutritional. People must eat a protein-free diet and get their required protein from special formulas that omit the dangerous amino acids. This diet is necessary for life because the disorder cannot be cured. Nevertheless, normal intelligence and physical health can be achieved if the diet is followed from birth—before damage is done.

GALACTOSEMIA

Galactosemia is another IEM that involves missing enzymes, but it is a disorder of carbohydrate metabolism, rather than protein metabolism. The missing enzymes are critical for metabolizing galactose. Galactose is a simple sugar that together with glucose forms the milk sugar lactose. Three different enzymes may be affected or missing. An infant born with galactosemia becomes seriously ill very quickly, whether being fed with breast milk or formula. Symptoms include loss of appetite, vomiting, lethargy, lack of weight gain, and seizures. Galactose builds up in the baby's body. If the condition is not treated, the brain, eyes, kidneys, and liver are permanently damaged.

The simple cure for galactosemia is to avoid any kind of milk product for life. Because galactose is not an essential nutrient, managing nutrition is not as difficult as it is with some other IEMs. Babies can be fed soy-based formula and given calcium supplements for growth and bone development. Children and adults must be careful to avoid any food that might contain galactose. They must read the labels of processed foods carefully so as to identify any ingredient (such as lactose, casein, curds, or milk solids) that may contain galactose. Other proteins, however, do not present a problem, so meat, fish, and eggs are acceptable. Many hospitals tests for galactosemia at birth because there can be severe consequences if it is not diagnosed immediately.

FRUCTOSEMIA

If the body is missing the enzyme called aldolase B, it is unable to break down fructose—a fruit sugar—and a disease known as fructosemia or fructose intolerance is the result. Like PKU and maple sugar urine disease, it is an inherited autosomal recessive disorder. A fructose-intolerant person cannot eat beet sugar, cane sugar or any foods to which fructose has been added as a sweetener, such as drinks or even baby foods. Sucrose, or table sugar, cannot be metabolized either. Often, fructose intolerance is diagnosed when a baby begins to eat baby food or drink formula. The sugars build up and damage the liver and kidneys. The body's cells cannot make glucose for energy. The earlier the disorder is discovered, the more normally the child can grow and develop.

Prevention of sickness and death depends on eliminating fructose and sucrose from the diet.

Avoiding sugars is easier than avoiding proteins. As a matter of fact, many children with fructose intolerance intensely dislike the taste of sweet foods and drinks. However, some nutritional inadequacies can develop because so many healthy foods—such as fruits, and even potatoes—contain fructose. People with hereditary fructosemia, however, can live normal, healthy lives if a nutritionist helps them to plan an appropriate diet.

DIETARY FRUCTOSE INTOLERANCE

Another kind of fructose intolerance is called fructose malabsorption or dietary fructose intolerance. It is not life threatening, not a childhood hereditary disease, and not an inborn error of metabolism. Instead, it seems to occur because the modern diets in wealthy countries often include extremely high levels of fructose added to processed foods. Although it appears to be caused by the diet, genetic variations may explain why some people are more likely than others to get it. Enzymes in the intestines apparently require equal amounts of glucose and fructose in order to metabolize fructose correctly. People who eat a lot of fructose may have an imbalance of fructose and glucose, and some of them cannot tolerate this condition. They develop uncomfortable gastrointestinal symptoms such as gas, bloating, belching, and diarrhea because the fructose in their foods is not absorbed well.

At the University of Iowa, Dr. Satish Rao has developed tests to diagnose dietary fructose intolerance and found evidence that people with this condition cannot consume more than 50 grams of fructose in a serving or meal. He believes that changes in diet, especially avoiding high-fructose corn syrup, can help relieve fructose intolerance, but these changes have to be permanent and lifelong. Dr. Rao is researching ways to develop an enzyme therapy to cure fructose malabsorption.

CYSTIC FIBROSIS

The failure to absorb nutrients is a major symptom of the most common autosomal recessive disease in European people: cystic fibrosis (CF). Although cystic fibrosis can occur among all ethnic groups, it is most common in Caucasians. This inherited disease affects about 30,000 people in the United States and approximately 70,000 people worldwide. The malfunctioning gene that causes cystic fibrosis disrupts the functioning of the body's exocrine glands. Exocrine glands secrete mucus and sweat. In cystic fibrosis, sweat becomes very salty and the body quickly can become depleted of salt, which disrupts the electrolyte balance. Mucus is supposed to keep organs slippery and moist, but in people with CF, mucus is thick and sticky. It clogs the lungs and blocks airways, causing lung infections. The thick mucus also blocks the ducts in the pancreas, keeping digestive enzymes from getting to the small intestine. Without these enzymes, the intestines cannot completely digest proteins and fats. Malnutrition and vitamin deficiency occur because nutrients, including fat-soluble vitamins, are not absorbed.

If the nutritional problems are not treated, children with CF fail to grow, are weak and lethargic, have weakened immune systems, and exhibit the same symptoms as starving children. About half of all children with CF who are not diagnosed in infancy have protein energy malnutrition. Because of their symptoms, people with CF have increased calorie and energy requirements. But even when their appetites are good, they cannot take in enough calories to maintain a healthy body weight and to grow and develop. Lung infections increase their metabolic rate and energy requirements. Yet, when people are ill with these infections, they often are vomiting and lose their appetites. Lungs can be badly damaged by repeated infections, and malnutrition makes people much more susceptible to lung infections. Respiratory failure and death can occur.

FIGURE 6.3 Tara Madison's daughter Ella was diagnosed with cystic fibrosis as a newborn. Cystic fibrosis is an autosomal recessive disease in which the malfunctioning gene that causes the disease disrupts the functioning of the body's exocrine glands. Ella, seen here at age 2 in 2007, has treatments twice a day with a vest that pounds her chest to loosen mucus, and she takes in medications with a nebulizer.

Today, aggressive nutritional intervention is a major part of CF treatment. CF cannot be prevented or cured, and reversal of lung problems is not possible. However, CF can be managed so that immune systems are strengthened, lung infections are reduced, bodies can grow, and people with CF can live healthier lives. First, nutritional management of CF requires replacing the missing enzymes. This is called pancreatic enzyme replacement therapy (PERT). Scientists have developed man-made versions of the blocked enzymes, which can be supplied in capsules. PERT improves digestion and absorption of foods and nutrients. The capsules are taken with every meal or snack. PERT does not work as well as natural pancreatic enzymes would, but it allows more fats and fat-soluble vitamins to be absorbed and greatly improves the digestion of proteins.

Energy needs for people with CF are high. Because fat is the most energy-dense nutrient, people with CF need to eat a diet that has about 40% of total calories from fat. (This is much higher than the maximum 25% recommended for people without CF.) Total energy intake must be higher than normal, too. Recommended calorie intake for health is anywhere from 10% higher to twice the estimated energy requirement (EAR) for healthy people. Because people with CF have trouble eating large amounts of food, they often resort to tricks, such as drinking half-and-half instead of milk, adding butter and cheese to vegetables, putting gravy on their meats and potatoes, and mixing extra eggs into hamburgers or casseroles. People with CF are encouraged to eat French fries, potato chips, ice cream, and pizza. If they still cannot get enough calories to maintain a healthy weight, feeding with a nasogastric tube may be necessary.

Vitamin and mineral supplements are a critical part of CF nutritional management. People with CF not only take a regular multivitamin, but also take extra doses of fat-soluble vitamins. The amount depends on a person's age, but those older than eight years old generally take an extra 10,000 units of vitamin A, 200 units of vitamin E, and at least 400 units of vitamin D every day. Extra vitamin K also is required in a supplement. Vitamin K helps blood to clot and helps enzymes to break down proteins. Vitamin K deficiency is very rare in the normal population, but it is a fat-soluble vitamin, so people with CF may not be able to absorb it in foods. People with CF also must eat a high-salt diet in the summer, because so much salt can be lost when they sweat. According to the Cystic Fibrosis Foundation, healthy lungs have more natural antioxidants than CF lungs. Because antioxidants help prevent infections and inflammation, some scientists believe that people with CF should take extra antioxidant supplements, too.

Nutritional management of CF is complex, but when people get enough calories, macronutrients, and micronutrients, they grow at a normal rate, go through puberty at the appropriate age, suffer fewer infections, and enjoy a good quality of life. Most nutritionists believe that people with CF live many years longer when adequate nutrition is supplied. When CF was first identified as a disease in 1938, most people died of it in infancy. Today, half the people with CF in the United States are adults. This improved outcome is due in large part to improved medical treatments of lung disease, but it is also due to aggressive prevention of malnutrition.

CELIAC DISEASE

Celiac disease, like cystic fibrosis, is a disease of malabsorption. It has a different cause, however, and requires different treatment. People with celiac disease cannot tolerate gluten, a protein in wheat, rye, and barley. Celiac disease is not an autosomal recessive disorder. It is believed to be caused by genetic variations that make the body react to gluten as if it is an invader. The immune system attacks the gluten, creating toxins that damage and destroy the villi that line the small intestine. Villi are tiny finger-like protrusions that allow nutrients to be absorbed into the bloodstream. Celiac disease is a kind of autoimmune disease. As the immune system responds to the presence of gluten, it ends up attacking the body itself. Once the intestine is damaged, macronutrients and micronutrients are not absorbed properly. The more villi that are damaged or destroyed, the worse the malabsorption is.

Celiac disease is a complex disorder, with different forms and varying symptoms. The "classic" form of the disease occurs in early childhood; it has severe effects when undiagnosed and untreated. Symptoms include diarrhea, failure to grow properly, anemia (a deficiency of red blood cells), and protein energy malnutrition. However, Dr. Michelle Pietzak, a celiac specialist writing in *Nutrition in the Prevention and Treatment of Disease*, calls

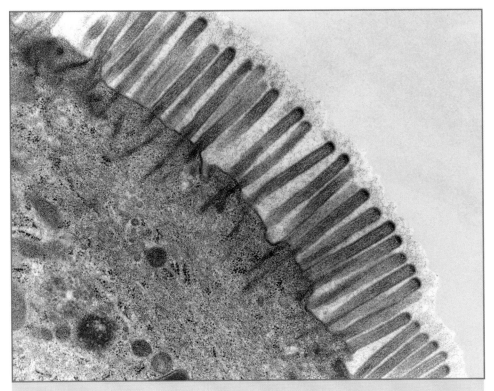

FIGURE 6.4 Villi in the small intestine allow nutrients to be absorbed into the blood stream. People with celiac disease have immune systems that attack gluten, creating toxins that damage or destroy these villi in the small intestine.

"classic" celiac disease just "the tip of the iceberg." She explains that "late-onset" celiac disease is a serious health problem in older children and adults, who are often misdiagnosed. Even when these people have pain, diarrhea, and weight loss, medical tests often fail to identify the gluten intolerance. Instead, people with celiac disease may be misdiagnosed with lactose intolerance, irritable bowel syndrome, or "abdominal pain of childhood." Other people with celiac disease may have joint pains, constipation, and vomiting. They, too, can be hard to diagnose because the medical recognition of late-onset celiac disease is relatively new. Some people may have no symptoms, because not enough villi have been destroyed to cause sickness. Diagnosis can be delayed for years, and during this delay, people's digestive systems are being damaged and nutritional deficiencies are putting their health at risk.

Celiac disease is most accurately diagnosed with endoscopy and a biopsy of the small intestine, along with a test of the person's response to gluten. To do the biopsy, a doctor threads a flexible instrument called an endoscope through the person's mouth and down to the small intestine. A camera on the endoscope allows the doctor to see any changes on the intestinal wall. Inflammation can be seen with the camera, and with a small tool on the endoscope, a tiny piece of tissue is cut and removed for further microscopic examination for damaged villi. However,

GENES THAT SAY "NO" BUT NOT "YES"

The specific genes that lead to the development of celiac disease have not yet been found, but some gene variations almost always occur in a person with celiac disease. These genes do not cause the disorder. Almost 40% of people have these variations, but not all of these people get celiac disease. Perhaps the genes are necessary for celiac disease to occur, but other factors are at play, too. The genes are called HLA (human leukocyte antigen) genes. HLA genes code for the ability of T cells in the immune system to find and destroy foreign invaders. Many variations of HLA genes occur normally, but two of them—labeled DQ2 and DQ8 by scientists—are found in 95% of people with celiac disease. A genetic test can determine whether someone has these HLA gene variations. If a person has neither DQ2 nor DQ8, the chance that he or she has celiac disease is extremely small. However, just because a person has one of these variations does not mean they have, or ever will have, celiac disease.

other disorders can damage villi, so the doctor cannot diagnose celiac disease without determining the person's response to gluten. The test and the treatment for celiac disease are the same: Eliminate gluten from the diet. In the vast majority of people with celiac disease, a gluten-free diet resolves all the symptoms, heals the small intestine, and ends the malabsorption of nutrients. In addition, any nutritional deficiencies can be reversed with supplements. The most likely deficiencies are of iron (a mineral that is a key component of red blood cells) and the fat-soluble vitamins A, E, D, and K. For most people, the effects of celiac disease can be prevented by avoiding gluten.

Gluten-free diets are not always easy to follow. People cannot eat anything made with wheat, rye, graham flour, bran, or barley. Many in the United States cannot eat oats either, because oats and wheat are often ground in the same mills, and the oats can be contaminated. Processed foods can contain hidden gluten. For example, products that list ingredients such as "hydrolyzed vegetable protein" or "flavorings" may contain gluten. Gluten may be used as flavoring in candy, sauces, soups, and salad dressings. It is even used as filler in some vitamin supplements and medicines. In Europe, Australia, and Canada, government standards require that food labels list gluten and that foods labeled "gluten-free" meet government criteria. In the United States, as of 2009, such standards are still under review by the Food and Drug Administration (FDA). Thus, many Americans have no way to be sure that a food is actually gluten free.

Coping with celiac disease is complicated and lifelong, but according to Pietzak, it is the only autoimmune disease with a known trigger. In that sense, people with celiac disease are fortunate. They know how to prevent the malabsorption and damage caused by gluten intolerance. They cannot change the gene variations that help lead to the intolerance. No one even knows all of the genes involved, much less how to make them function normally. But people with celiac disease usually can recover completely with the appropriate nutritional intervention.

FIGURE 6.5 People who cannot tolerate gluten cannot eat foods that are made with wheat, rye, graham flour, bran, or barley. Gluten-free products, like these, can now be found in many mainstream grocery stores.

REVIEW

Unhealthy diet choices are not the only reason for nutritional deficiencies. Some people are born with genetic differences and mutations that make them unable to absorb or metabolize certain nutrients. These people have specialized nutritional requirements that must be met to prevent disability or death. Inborn errors of metabolism (IEMs) are serious diseases caused by defective recessive genes. They are rare diseases, but some of the best known are phenylketonuria, maple sugar urine disease, galactosemia, and fructosemia. In each IEM, missing enzymes prevent the metabolism of nutrients and result in toxic buildups and other severe problems in the body. Prevention of disability and death requires lifelong avoidance of the nutrient for which there is no enzyme, while still maintaining a healthy diet. Cystic fibrosis and celiac disease are disorders that involve malabsorption of macronutrients and micronutrients. Protein energy malnutrition is common. In cystic fibrosis, malabsorption occurs because the pancreatic digestive enzymes are blocked and cannot reach the small intestine. Specialized nutritional intervention is required for weight maintenance, micronutrient deficiencies, and strengthening the immune system. In celiac disease, malabsorption occurs because the body cannot tolerate gluten. A gluten-free diet allows the intestinal damage to heal, and reverses nutritional deficiencies. In both cases, achieving optimal nutrition is challenging but of critical importance to overall health.

7

NUTRIGENOMICS

People with metabolic disorders or inherited diseases are not the only ones who have variations and mutations in their genes: Everyone does. Vulnerability to disease and how our metabolisms work depends partly upon the gene variations we have inherited. How much of a nutrient we need to prevent disease and achieve optimum health may be as unique to each person as appearance and personality. Our particular set of genes and all of our DNA is called our **genome**. Each individual's genome is unique, although we share many similarities with others. An emerging science named nutrigenomics focuses on the interaction between nutrition and our genes. Its ultimate goal is to someday tailor each person's diet to his or her specific genetic needs. With personalized nutritional advice, each person could live a longer life and have fewer diseases.

NUTRIENTS AND GENE INTERACTIONS

The idea that we should eat what is best for our genes is a logical one and based on a good deal of evidence. No one can genetically tailor people's diets today, but nutrigenomics scientists are working toward a future when they will know enough about nutrients and genes to make the idea a reality. In a 2008 interview with *Whole Foods* magazine, nutrigenomics expert Dr. Jim Kaput explained what he said are "the five guiding precepts" of nutrigenomics research. They are:

- Common dietary chemicals act on the human genome, either directly or indirectly, to alter **gene expression** (the translation or interpretation of information coded in the gene's DNA) or structure.
- Under certain circumstances and in some individuals, diet can be a serious risk factor for a number of diseases.
- Some diet-regulated genes (and their normal, common variants) are likely to play a role in the onset, incidence, progression and/or severity of chronic diseases.
- The degree to which diet influences the balance between healthy and disease states may depend on an individual's genetic makeup.
- Dietary intervention based on knowledge of nutritional requirement, nutritional status, and **genotype** (each individual's particular set of genes; i.e., "individualized nutrition") can be used to prevent, mitigate or cure chronic disease.

NUTRIENTS AS GENE SWITCHES

In 2000, scientists Randy Jirtle and Robert Waterland experimented with the effect of nutrients on gene expression and disease with some specially bred laboratory mice. The mice carried a gene known as the agouti gene. The gene made them yellow instead of brown, caused them to be ravenously hungry and become obese, and made them susceptible to diseases such as diabetes and cancer. The scientists mated the agouti mice and, when the mothers were pregnant, Jirtle and Waterland fed them food supplements rich

LOSE THE COFFEE AND (MAYBE) SAVE YOUR BONES

Osteoporosis is a bone-thinning disease that affects many elderly women. Over time, their bones become less dense, and their risk of fractures is high. Yet not all older women develop osteoporosis, and some have the disease much more severely than others. Scientists believe that the reason for this difference may lie in the genes. One gene is called the vitamin D receptor gene, or VDR. It codes for the receptors that bind vitamin D in the cells of many organs in the body. When these receptors bind vitamin D, they are activated to regulate the balance of calcium in the body. This enables the body to metabolize and absorb calcium and to build strong bones. People cannot absorb calcium without enough vitamin D. Scientists have identified variations of the VDR gene that are labeled TT (normal) and tt (mutated). People with the tt variation who also drink a lot of coffee are at increased risk for bone weakening, calcium loss in the bones, and osteoporosis. Researchers theorize that the caffeine interacts with VDR, decreasing its expression, which reduces the number of vitamin D receptors in cells. This, in turn, decreases calcium absorption. Women with the TT variation are much less affected by consuming caffeine. Someday, when everyone's genotype can be tested for disease risk, women with the tt variation will be advised to limit caffeine intake to help prevent osteoporosis. For now, scientists suggest that all older women keep coffee intake below 16 ounces (473 milliliters) per day, tea intake below 32 ounces (946 mL), and caffeinated soda below 12 ounces (355 mL).

in methyl donors. Methyl donors are nutrient chemicals found in some B vitamins and common in foods such as garlic, beets, and onions. The nutrient chemicals attached to the agouti genes in the developing baby agouti mice and acted like a chemical switch for the genes. The genes and DNA coding were still there, but gene expression was turned off. The baby mice were born brown, had normal appetites, and lived long, disease-free lives.

Writing about this experiment in a 2006 *Discover* magazine article, journalist Ethan Watters notes, "More and more, researchers are finding that an extra bit of a vitamin, a brief exposure to a toxin, even an added dose of mothering...[can] alter the software of our genes." In the case of the baby agouti mice, it was a nutrient that changed the **phenotype** (the looks, behaviors, and traits) of the mice, even though the genotype was not changed. Mice are not people, and people do not have agouti genes, but nutrigenomics experts believe that different nutrients can act as switches that turn genes on and off in humans, too.

Scientists now know that not all nutrients are metabolized for energy or maintaining cell functions. Some chemicals from nutrients, such as the methyl donors, may actually prevent gene variations from causing harm or leading to disease. Jirtle and Waterland's experiment is a good example of how a nutrient might affect cell activity and gene expression, whether that nutrient is a macronutrient, a micronutrient, or another nutrient chemical. In Watter's *Discover* article, Jirtle is quoted as saying "Now everything we do—everything we eat or smoke—can effect our gene expression and that of future generations."

NUTRIENTS AND GENE EXPRESSION

According to researchers at the Nutritional Genomics Center at the University of California at Davis, chemicals from nutrients can affect gene expression directly (A) or indirectly (B and C). Nutrient chemicals may attach to genes directly (A). They may be metabolized, and alter other molecules that regulate genes and

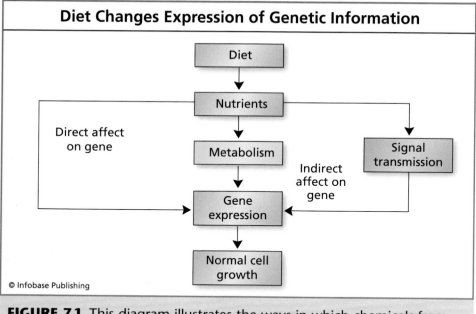

FIGURE 7.1 This diagram illustrates the ways in which chemicals from nutrients can affect gene expression both directly and indirectly.

signal cells (B), or they may activate or inhibit chemical pathways in a cell (signal transduction) (C).

NUTRIENTS AND DNA REPAIR

Some nutrients may also act to protect the genome from damage. DNA is constantly replicating itself, and thousands of mistakes are made each day as a result. If the mistakes were not fixed, the genome eventually would be irreparably damaged, and we would develop diseases or die. Genes, nutrients, and lifestyle (exercise, smoking, environmental pollutants) determine how well repair takes place and how much damage occurs. Nutrigenomic scientists suspect that cell damage that is not effectively repaired is the cause of many diseases, such as cancer. For example, in a 2007 experiment, special mice with genes that predisposed them to skin cancer were exposed to UVB radiation, similar to radiation from the sun. Half the mice were given a component of B vitamins called inositol in their drinking water. These mice developed far fewer skin tumors than those who received no inositol—23% versus 51%. The researcher, A.M. Shamsuddin, suggested that this result could have meaning for people who are airline pilots or frequent fliers. They might need more inositol in their diets to protect them from skin cancer. The experiment seemed to demonstrate one way that nutrients can protect DNA when the environment is harmful.

NUTRIGENOMICS SAYS...

Studies such as Shamsuddin's, however, never yield results of 100% certainty. All the mice receiving inositol did not avoid tumors. All the mice eating a regular diet did not develop cancer. Whether with mice or human cells or people, scientists do not discover "magic bullets" or simple answers that explain how to prevent disease. Part of the reason is that individuals respond differently to the same diet. The trick for scientists is identifying both the specific genes and the nutrients that determine health and disease.

For the most part, Dr. Kaput explains, nutrigenomic principles of disease prevention are most easily applied to groups of people who share similar metabolic genetic profiles and lifestyles. These similar profiles may be due to having the same ancestry or belonging to the same ethnic group. Some gene variants occur more frequently in one ethnic group than another. However, there are no genes exclusive to one race or ethnic group. All groups of humans are susceptible to the same gene variations.

SIMILAR ANCESTRY, SIMILAR GENETIC PROBLEMS

One well-established gene variant, for example, occurs on the angiotensin gene, called ANG. One variation in ANG increases a person's risk for high blood pressure. This gene variant occurs most

TABLE 7.1 MICRONUTRIENTS AND DNA

Serious health problems can be caused by deficiencies in selected micro-nutrients (due to decreased intake or increased individual need) and resulting DNA damage.

Micronutrient Deficiency	DNA Damage	Health Effects
Folic acid	Chromosome breaks	Colon cancer; heart disease; brain dysfunction
Vitamin C	DNA oxidation	Cataracts; cancer
Vitamin E	DNA oxidation	Colon cancer; heart disease; immune dysfunction
Iron	DNA breaks; DNA oxidation	DNA breaks
Zinc	Chromosome breaks; DNA oxidation	Brain and immune system dysfunction; cancer
Niacin	Disables DNA repair	Neurological symptoms; memory loss

Adapted from "Table 1: Micronutrient Deficiency and DNA Damage" in "Micronutrients," The NCMHD Center of Excellence for Nutritional Genomics, UC Davis. Available Online. URL: http://nutrigenomics.ucdavis.edu/nutrigenomics/index.cfm?objectid=9688A280-65B3-C1E7-02E9FCDABDD84C68.

commonly in African Americans. People with this gene variant can control high blood pressure with a low-salt diet. About 73% of African Americans are salt sensitive and will be helped by such a diet. Many people of European ancestry have the same variation in the same gene. Those people, too, will be helped by a low-salt diet. But the same diet will not help people with high blood pressure due to another cause. Some people, for instance, need a diet rich in calcium to lower blood pressure. If a physician knows a person has the ANG variant, he or she can better treat high blood pressure.

The thrifty genes that may lead to metabolic syndrome, obesity, diabetes, and heart disease also seem to vary among populations. Although these gene variations affect many people of European ancestry, they are even more common among certain indigenous populations, such as Native Americans, Polynesians, and aboriginal peoples in Australia and Canada. Among many of these peoples, the high-fat, high-sugar diets of wealthy Europeans have had devastating health effects. For example, the Pima Indians of Arizona have the highest incidence of type 2 diabetes of any group of people in the world. Out of 11,000 Pima Indians living along the Gila River, half have diabetes and 95% are overweight. Nutrigenomics researchers are trying to identify the genes that cause this reaction to specific diets. If they succeed, they will be able to warn vulnerable people and recommend appropriate diets to prevent the chronic diseases caused by the interaction of thrifty genes and diet. This would help to reduce some of the health disparities between ethnic groups.

GENE VARIANTS AND NUTRIGENOMICS SUCCESS

Although obesity and disease may be the result of nutrient intake that triggers the expression of thrifty genes, other nutrients can prevent disease. Perhaps some of these nutrients could even partially offset the effects of thrifty genes. In 2009, Olha Kyhmenets and a scientific team reported on a study of virgin olive oil. The researchers fed a group of healthy men and women virgin olive oil for three weeks as their major dietary source of fat. The participants were given extra olive oil as a food supplement, too. Then, each person's genome was examined for changes in genes. The researchers were looking for evidence about genes that are believed to control cholesterol levels and the onset of arteriosclerosis. Both of these conditions are associated with an increased risk of heart attacks. The participants' genes did react to the olive oil. A total of 10 genes showed differences in expression, and some of them were genes that control the metabolism of fatty acids and lipids. Other scientists, in other studies, have found that virgin olive oil can reduce DNA oxidation and free radicals. DNA damage in blood cells and blood vessel walls is known to occur with arteriosclerosis, and two of the genes that Kyhmenets identified are part of the body's DNA-repair system. A single study does not prove that everyone needs to eat olive oil to repair DNA and prevent arteriosclerosis, but the research team does assert that they have evidence that olive oil can alter the expression of genes.

Recently, scientists have identified a gene referred to as MTHFR, which codes for an enzyme that helps break down amino acids. When this enzyme doesn't work properly, an amino acid called homocysteine builds up in the blood. Increased blood levels of homocysteine increase a person's risk of heart disease and blood vessel disease. In 15% to 20% of people of European ancestry, a variation of the MTHFR gene makes the enzyme work less efficiently. People with this variant have high levels of homocysteine in their blood, unless they are taking folic acid supplements. The folic acid normalizes the metabolism and ensures good gene expression.

PERSONALIZED DIETS TAILORED TO GENOTYPES

Today, scientists have been able to identify about 20 genes with variants that may make people have an increased need for certain nutrients. However, humans probably have between 20,000 and 30,000 genes, and scientists are unsure of all the nutrient interactions that may be important even for the 20 genes they have identified. Nevertheless, as nutrigenomics research progresses, scientists are sure that the time will come when individual genomes can be tested, people will be told their risk for a variety of diseases, and diets can be planned for the specific nutrient intake that will sustain optimal health. Each person will have a personalized nutritional plan, with specific foods to eat.

Raymond L. Rodriguez is the director of nutrigenomics research at the University of California, Davis. In an interview with *Technology Review* (a magazine put out by the Massachusetts Institute of Technology), he explains, "You bring two things to

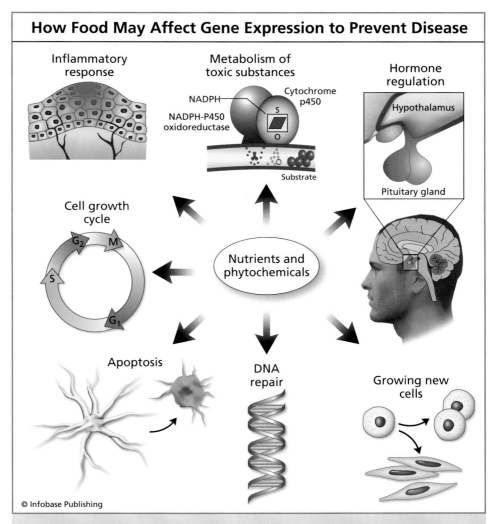

How Food May Affect Gene Expression to Prevent Disease

Inflammatory response

Metabolism of toxic substances

NADPH

NADPH-P450 oxidoreductase

Cytochrome p450

S

O

Substrate

Hormone regulation

Hypothalamus

Pituitary gland

Cell growth cycle

G_2 M

S

G_1

Nutrients and phytochemicals

Apoptosis

DNA repair

Growing new cells

© Infobase Publishing

FIGURE 7.2 It appears that some nutrients and phytochemicals could play a role in preventing cancer by interacting with the genes that control many biological processes, from DNA repair to hormone regulation.

the table: your appetite and your genotype. When you consume a food, your genes are like a Christmas tree, red and green lights that flip on and off and flicker back and forth. My Christmas lights differ from yours and flicker at a different rate. Over time, depending on your types of genes and how frequently they're turned on and off, you'll either be healthy or in a disease state." So, with nutrigenomics, some people with genes that cause accumulation of bad cholesterol in their blood could prevent heart disease by eating a low-fat diet. Others, with different genes, will not decrease their overall fat intake. Instead, they will eat a diet high in polyunsaturated fats, such as liquid vegetable oils, nuts, and fatty fish. Still others will have genes that protect them from high cholesterol levels. They could eat all the bacon, butter, and saturated fats that they want.

Some people might have a gene variant that encourages weight gain with high-carbohydrate diets, and, thus, they may need to minimize their intake of high-carbohydrate foods. Others may have genes that slow down their metabolism, and, thus, might need to avoid weight gain by eating foods (such as flax seeds, nuts, and beans) that signal their genes to increase metabolism. Some people will be advised to avoid alcohol; for others, a daily glass of wine will be recommended. Individuals with gene variants that put them at risk for some cancers might be urged to eat oily fish, take extra calcium supplements, and eat vegetables rich in antioxidants.

DO YOU REALLY WANT TO KNOW?

Nutrigenomics could help everyone live up to his or her genetic potential and avoid chronic and life-threatening diseases, but some experts imagine ethical problems when personalized nutrition recommendations become a reality. Everyone would have to undergo DNA testing and genome mapping. Each person would know his or her gene variations and disease risks. Such knowledge might not be beneficial. The European Nutrigenomics Organisation (NuGO) suggests that ethical considerations will have to be a strong component of gene testing. An article on the NuGO Web site cites the example of a gene mutation that occurs in about 2% of the British population. It is associated with a high risk of early heart disease and blood vessel disease. People with this gene variant are not certain to develop heart problems at a young age, but many do, and a low-fat diet can reduce the risk. An individual with this risk might want to know about the problem so as to

SCIENCE OR QUACKERY?

Scientists say that nutrigenomics holds promise for the future, but it is not yet ready for public consumption. Nevertheless, several for-profit companies offer genetic testing, individualized diet plans, and nutritional supplement recommendations as the way to prevent diseases. Most medical professionals and nutrigenomics researchers consider these claims dubious at best. GeneWatch UK has called claims for individualized treatment plans for disease prevention misleading and unethical. This British nonprofit organization explains that gene/nutrient interactions are still poorly understood and that lifestyles are much more important than genotypes in determining who will get a specific disease. They say that such companies are playing on people's fears in order to make money. In 2005 and 2006, the U.S. Government Accountability Office tried an experiment. It sent 12 genetic samples to 4 companies that advertised individual genetic profile testing and nutritional plans. Nine of the samples sent were from the same baby, but the companies offered different recommendations for these identical samples. Two of the companies offered expensive supplements to prevent future disease. These supplements were the same as nutritional supplements that could be bought in any store, but they cost 30 times more. The government researchers concluded that the genetic tests and recommendations were inaccurate, of no medical value, and predicted future disease risk unscientifically.

change his or her diet to reduce the risk of heart disease, strokes, and arteriosclerosis. However, this same gene mutation is also linked with a 60% greater risk of developing Alzheimer's disease. The NuGO site notes: "Currently, there is no means of preventing or curing Alzheimer's disease, and it is not clear whether modification of the individual's dietary lipids also reduces their risk of Alzheimer's disease." Perhaps not everyone would want to face the fact that a degenerative, incurable disease lies in the future, especially if no treatments are available to slow the memory loss.

If the results of genetic testing were not kept private, there could be serious problems, too. Employers could refuse to hire people with certain genotypes. Insurance companies might refuse coverage to people with certain gene variations. Perhaps employers or insurance companies would try to require people to be genotyped or to follow personalized nutrition plans recommended by nutrigenomics experts. These are not desirable results, argues NuGO. NuGO says that everyone should have the option to reject genotyping or ignore nutritional advice based on genotype. People should be free to make their own choices, and no one should be discriminated against because of those nutritional or informational choices or because of their genes. Nutrigenomics is a science of much promise, but some ethical peril. Nutrigenomic researchers believe that guidelines and ethical education will be necessary in the future to ensure that this young and emerging science does not harm the very people it hopes to help.

REVIEW

Nutrigenomics is the study of the interaction between nutrients and genes. It is the effort to identify the relationship of each individual's genome to his or her nutritional requirements, and thereby reduce the risk of chronic disease and increase optimum health. Nutrigenomics is a new science, but already, researchers have evidence that nutrients can act upon genes—influencing gene expression, repairing DNA errors, and protecting the genome from damage. Common gene variations among different groups of people can increase the need for certain nutrients or increase the risk for certain diseases. Diseases that may be dependent on genetic variations and amenable to nutritional intervention include diabetes, cardiovascular disease, obesity, and cancers. Nutritional intervention tailored to genotypes could prevent these diseases and help people achieve optimum health. In the future, nutrigenomics experts expect to be able to plan individual, specific diets with recommended food choices based on genetic need. When this expectation becomes reality, ethical issues about the use of genotyping and the freedom of each individual to act upon nutrigenomic recommendations will have to be addressed.

EMERGING SCIENCE

Nutrigenomics is not yet a reality, but modern research is defining the complicated relationship between nutrition and disease prevention at a rapid pace. Researchers are starting to understand how micronutrients affect health. They also have found substances in foods that may be critical to health, though they are not recognized as essential nutrients. How important these discoveries are is still controversial, but many nutritional experts and medical professionals are already making dietary recommendations based on mounting evidence of the connection between nutrients and disease.

SUPER VITAMIN D

In a 2008 newspaper article, Dr. Craig Bowron called vitamin D a nutritional "superstar." Not only is the vitamin involved in calcium absorption and the prevention of rickets, it is of vital importance to many body systems, including the expression of about 2,000 genes, about 10% of the human genome. Researchers say that it is clear that people need ample vitamin D. Yet, most people are deficient in the vitamin, though it is made at high levels in sun-exposed skin.

HOW VITAMIN D WORKS

Technically, vitamin D is not a vitamin. It is a family of chemical compounds that act more like a hormone. When people are exposed to sunlight, ultraviolet B (UVB) radiation is absorbed by their skin. In the skin is a chemical called provitamin D3. It is a kind of cholesterol. It reacts to the UVB radiation to form previtamin D3. Over several hours, previtamin D3 is changed into D3, or **cholecalciferol**. This is released into the bloodstream, where it binds with a protein and is carried to the liver. Because D3 is fat soluble, it can be stored in the liver. There, it can be converted into other compounds that travel to the kidneys. The kidneys make the active form of vitamin D, which is then used elsewhere in the body. This fits the definition of a hormone: a chemical made by one part of the body to be used by other parts. Active vitamin D made in the kidneys circulates in the blood and is used by many other body systems.

Instead of being converted by the kidneys, some vitamin D compounds bind directly with receptors in body cells. Scientists do not know exactly how vitamin D3 is converted to active vitamin D in this system, but they have found vitamin D receptors in many organs, such as the brain, pancreas, prostate, breasts, and colon, as well as in immune system cells.

SOURCES OF VITAMIN D

With enough sunshine, animal and human bodies can make their own active vitamin D. Few foods naturally contain vitamin D. Wild cod often have large quantities of vitamin D in their livers. So, cod liver oil is one of the few food sources of vitamin D. Egg yolks have a little vitamin D, as does butter. Some plants make a different form of vitamin D from ultraviolet light. It is called vitamin D2, or **ergocalciferol**. Both vitamin D2 and D3 can be converted by human bodies into active vitamin D, but D2 is not absorbed as efficiently as D3. It takes three times more vitamin D2 over a longer period of time to get adequate levels in the blood than it does for D3. Often, the vitamin D added to milk, breakfast cereals, and cheese or provided in multivitamin supplements is ergocalciferol.

In theory, the best kind of vitamin D is D3, made from the sun, but modern people just do not get enough sun exposure to avoid deficiency. Our original human ancestors evolved in Africa, wore little or no clothing, and were exposed to warm, direct sunlight most of the year. They acquired ample vitamin D from sunshine. Today, on the other hand, people live in northern latitudes, cover

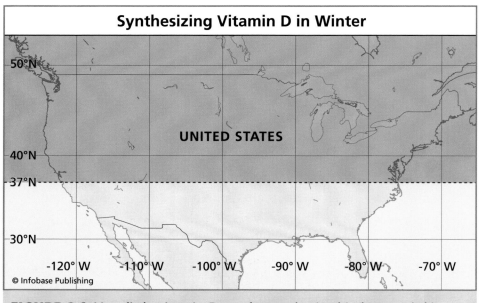

FIGURE 8.1 Very little vitamin D can be synthesized in humans' skin between November and February at latitudes north of 37 degrees on a map.

up with clothing, inhabit smoggy cities, and spend much time indoors. In addition, light-skinned people absorb UVB radiation more easily than dark-skinned people. About 20 to 30 minutes of summertime exposure is enough for a fair-skinned person (with face, arms, legs, and part of the torso bare), but someone with darker skin may need up to three hours to make enough vitamin D for good health. Older people also absorb UVB radiation less easily than younger people. People who wear sunscreen to protect against skin cancer block UVB absorption. Even glass windows prevent the synthesis of active vitamin D. Choosing shade over direct sunlight reduces vitamin D absorption by 60%. In winter, the angle of the sun prevents absorption for everyone in temperate climates.

VITAMIN D INSUFFICIENCY

Vitamin D insufficiency is now seen as a public health epidemic in much of the world. In the United States, 40% to 60% of the population does not have enough vitamin D in their blood. Among children, teens, and young adults, the incidence of insufficiency is 70%. Worldwide, about 1 billion people are deficient. Because it is impossible to know how much vitamin D a person makes when exposed to the sun, RDAs for vitamin D have never been determined. Instead, an adequate intake (AI)—a best guess—for vitamin D to ensure healthy bones is set by the National Academy of Sciences. Because vitamin D is known to be toxic at high levels, the AI is set quite low. The amount varies by age and gender, but for infants, children, and teens, the AI is currently 5 micrograms or 200 International Units (IU).

Many medical researchers and scientists believe that this amount is grossly inadequate and that the risk of toxicity is exaggerated. In 2008, the American Academy of Pediatrics (AAP) doubled its recommendation for infants, children, and teens to 400 IU of vitamin D daily. Dr. Frank Greer, the chairman of the AAP's National Committee on Nutrition, explained, "We are doubling the recommended amount of vitamin D children need each day because evidence has shown this could have life-long health benefits. Supplementation is important because most children will not get enough vitamin D through diet alone." In 2008, the American Medical Association (AMA) also requested that AIs for vitamin D be reviewed and reassessed. In August 2009, the National Academy of Sciences' Institute of Medicine began an official review of the U.S. government's recommended daily intake of vitamin D.

Many researchers not only agree that AIs must be revised, but also already recommend large doses of vitamin D supplements. Grassroots Health: D Action is an organization of vitamin D scientists who recommend that medical doctors test every patient

WAY TOO MUCH OF A GOOD THING

Vitamin D can be toxic, or poisonous, to the body in very high supplement doses. (The body naturally prevents any toxicity from sun exposure by stopping its manufacture of vitamin D when levels threaten to become excessive.) The supplemental dose level thought to be toxic is about 50,000 IU. For some people, this level can be toxic within a matter of days, but for others it may take decades before symptoms appear. Vitamin D toxicity causes high levels of calcium in the blood, which can severely damage bones, tissues, and kidneys. Symptoms of poisoning include constipation, nausea, lethargy, mental confusion, high blood pressure, dehydration, and disturbances in heart rhythm. Vitamin D toxicity can be serious, but usually the only treatment required is to stop taking the supplements completely. In severe cases, the person may also have to avoid sun exposure until blood levels of vitamin D return to normal. Toxicity occurs because vitamin D is a fat-soluble vitamin, meaning it can be stored in the body. Excess amounts of water-soluble vitamins are excreted in the urine. Any fat-soluble vitamin can be toxic at high levels.

for adequate blood levels of vitamin D. Sixteen of its member scientists issued an action statement recommending 2,000 IU, in the form of D3 supplements, as a minimum intake for almost every adult. The scientists argue that the risk of insufficiency far outweighs the risk of toxicity. Another advocacy organization, the California-based Vitamin D Council, quotes journalist Mike Adams as saying, "Vitamin D is, without question, the miracle nutrient of the century."

THE IMPORTANCE OF VITAMIN D

Why are so many scientists and doctors excited about vitamin D? Not only are most people deficient, but numerous respected scientific studies have demonstrated that low levels of vitamin D are linked to many diseases and disorders. Osteoporosis, the disease of weakened bones common among the elderly, and osteomalacia, a rickets-like disease in adults, are both linked to low levels of vitamin D. Almost 3,000 studies link vitamin D with cancer prevention. Insufficiency of this vitamin has also been implicated in diabetes, autoimmune diseases (multiple sclerosis, chronic muscle fatigue, and fibromyalgia), heart disease, strokes, kidney disease, and malabsorption disorders (for example, celiac disease and cystic fibrosis). There is evidence that it is associated with resistance to infections, such as influenza and tuberculosis. Some scientists even believe that further research will prove a connection between the brain and vitamin D that explains conditions such as depression and autism.

Vitamin D is essential for strong bones and teeth throughout life. It helps promote calcium absorption, and calcium is the major building block of bones and teeth. With osteoporosis, as with many disorders, the foundations for prevention are laid down with ample nutrition in childhood and adolescence, even though the disease does not appear until middle or old age. Nevertheless, nutritionists already recommend 1,000 IU for people at risk for osteoporosis. This dosage is especially helpful in winter or when people are confined to nursing homes, where they rarely get enough sun exposure. Vitamin D not only seems to strengthen bones and reduce the risk of fractures, it also increases muscle strength and improves balance. Studies have shown that increased

TABLE 8.1 DISEASES CURRENTLY SUSPECTED OF HAVING A RELATIONSHIP TO VITAMIN D INSUFFICIENCY

- Skeletal diseases
  - Rickets
  - Osteomalacia
  - Osteoporosis
- Cancer
  - Breast
  - Prostate
  - Colon
- Bacterial Infections
  - Tuberculosis
- Autoimmune diseases
  - Multiple Sclerosis
  - Diabetes (type 1 and type 2)
  - Other: irritable bowel syndrome, rheumatoid arthritis, lupus
- Cardiovascular disease
- High blood pressure
  - Atherosclerosis
- Malabsorption disorders
  - Crohn's disease
  - Celiac disease
  - Cystic fibrosis

Source: Coulston, Ann M. and Boushey, Carol J. (eds.). Nutrition in the Prevention and Treatment of Disease. *Burlington, MA: Elsevier, 2008. Adapted from Chapter 43, p. 823.*

vitamin D intake is associated with better balance, walking, and standing up from a chair in people 65 years and older.

In people with type 2 diabetes, several studies have concluded that high levels of vitamin D reduce insulin resistance in the cells and increase the insulin produced by the pancreas. It has been shown to improve the symptoms of autoimmune diseases in which the immune system attacks body systems as if they are foreign invaders. In other studies, ample vitamin D levels have improved the symptoms of people with congestive heart failure and reduced the risk of heart disease and heart attacks. In one 2009 study, researchers even discovered that ample vitamin D intake in pregnant women reduced the risk of asthma and allergies in their infants in later childhood.

VITAMIN D AND CANCER

Many studies suggest that vitamin D can prevent cancer. Inadequate vitamin D has been shown to increase the risk for colon cancer, and daily supplements of 1,000 IU are associated with a 50% decrease in the incidence of colon cancer. In one four-year study of about 1,200 older women, half the women were given calcium supplements and half were given calcium and vitamin D supplements. Researchers wanted to see which group developed less osteoporosis, but they were startled to discover that after only one year, the women taking vitamin D had only 25% of the risk of developing cancer, compared with the other group. In another large study, women taking 1,000 IU of vitamin D every day decreased their risk of breast cancer by 50%.

No one is sure how much vitamin D is needed in supplements or fortified foods. Many scientists advocate getting vitamin D the natural way—through sunshine. Some even argue that the use of sunscreen is increasing the risk of cancer in the United States population. Writing in *Nutrition in the Prevention and Treatment of Disease*, nutrition professor Susan J. Whiting and her colleagues conclude, "Although sun exposure increases the risk of developing skin cancer, it has the potential to reduce the risk of developing more severe forms of cancer."

Other scientists, however, argue for increased food fortification and use of vitamin D3 supplements by almost everyone. Dr. Cedric Garland is one of the scientists of D Action and the lead investigator of a new five-year study to determine cancer rates in people with adequate vitamin D in their blood. He believes that vitamin D protects against cancer by damaging the ability of cancer cells to stick together and communicate with one another. This probably happens because vitamin D influences gene expression. In a study published in 2009 in the journal *Annals of Epidemiology*, Garland and his scientific team argue that everyone should take 2,000 IU of vitamin D3 year round. He explains that if everyone in the United States and Canada had adequate blood levels of vitamin D and calcium, 58,000 cases of breast cancer and 49,000 cases of colon cancer would be prevented every year. Also, he says, fatalities in people who are already diagnosed with cancer would be cut in half.

DISEASE PREVENTION AND PHYTOCHEMICALS

Vitamin D is not the only nutrient strongly linked to cancer prevention. Some researchers have estimated that 35% to 75% of all cancerous tumors are linked to less than optimal nutrition. In addition, the known essential micronutrients and macronutrients may not be enough to support optimum health and prevent disease. Scientists have discovered that non-nutrient chemicals in foods play a large role in maintaining body functions.

Phytochemicals are chemicals in plant foods that may be important for health, but are not recognized as essential nutrients. A single fruit or vegetable may have hundreds of phytochemicals. Plants produce phytochemicals to protect themselves, and emerging science suggests that these chemicals can protect health and prevent disease in humans, too. More than 1,000 phytochemicals have been isolated and identified, and there are likely thousands more. Some seem to have antioxidant effects. Some seem to be antibacterial. Others act as hormones or affect enzyme functioning. Some may change DNA instructions in cancer cells. Others may bind to the walls of cells, strengthening them and protecting them from damage.

FIGURE 8.2 Phytochemicals are found in plant foods and are not recognized as essential nutrients, but scientists are discovering that in addition to being beneficial to plants, they may protect health and prevent disease in humans, too.

Researchers are still identifying phytochemicals and working to understand their roles in human health. Some major classes already discovered are flavonoids, carotenoids, and isoflavones. Genistein, a plant estrogen, is an isoflavone. It is similar to the estrogen hormone in people. Drs. Jirtle and Waterland joined a research team that used genistein in a 2006 agouti mice experiment and discovered that it, too, could change the coat color of baby mice and reduce their risk of obesity when it was fed to mothers during pregnancy. Scientists are still researching whether genistein might protect people from certain diseases and whether high amounts are good or bad for humans. Few foods, except soy, provide high levels of genistein.

CAROTENOIDS

Carotenoids make the orange, yellow, and red colors in plants such as carrots, tomatoes, and pumpkins. In plants, these chemicals have antioxidant effects, and they could act as antioxidants in humans as well. The body converts a carotenoid called beta-carotene into vitamin A. Some studies suggest that supplements of beta-carotene improve immune system functioning, but this may be because vitamin A is important for the immune system. Beta-carotene also can prevent vitamin A deficiency. Other studies, however, have found that beta-carotene supplements might increase the risk of lung cancer in smokers and former smokers. For now, scientists say that not enough is known about beta-carotene's action to recommend supplements.

Lycopene, the carotenoid found in tomatoes, seems to be of value in cancer prevention. Several studies conclude that diets rich in tomatoes, especially concentrated as sauce or paste, reduce the risk of prostate cancer in men. Lutein, a carotenoid in green, leafy vegetables, may protect against eye diseases, such as cataracts and macular degeneration (a cause of blindness in the elderly). Lutein is found in the retina of the eye, where it absorbs blue light. It may prevent eye damage caused by light exposure. In four studies, researchers found that people who ate diets rich in spinach, kale, and broccoli were less likely to develop cataracts than other people. However, the researchers were not sure if this result was due to the lutein or to other factors. Studies about the value of lutein and other carotenoids in preventing disease are ongoing.

FLAVONOIDS

Flavonoids are phytochemicals found in tea, red wine, fruits, vegetables, beans, and peas. Scientists believe they may be important as antioxidants, to help cells signal one another, and for gene expression. Cell signaling may be particularly important with cancer cells. Flavonoids may help to prevent cancer cells from multiplying and aid the signals that lead to cell death (apoptosis).

BROCCOLI SPROUTS

At The Johns Hopkins University, a team of researchers found evidence that broccoli sprouts might help to prevent stomach cancer. A phytochemical in broccoli sprouts, sulforaphane, acts as an antibiotic. *Helicobacter pylori* bacteria cause infections in the stomach that can lead to stomach cancer. Researchers treated 48 Japanese men and women who were infected with *H. pylori*. Half were given 2.5 ounces (70 grams) of broccoli sprouts daily for eight weeks; the other half ate the same amount of alfalfa sprouts. At the end of the experiment, the people eating alfalfa sprouts had the same levels of H. pylori infection as they did at the beginning of the test. Those who ate broccoli sprouts showed a significant decrease in levels of *H. pylori* bacteria and inflammation in their stomachs.

Scientists have found that diets rich in flavonoids can reduce cancer risk in animals. So far, human studies are contradictory. Two European studies found a reduced risk of lung cancer in people who ate flavonoid-rich diets. An American study showed a reduced risk of rectal cancer in women who drank flavonoid-rich tea. However, other studies in humans have not found the same results. Although scientists continue to research the connection between flavonoids and cancer, the work is difficult because flavonoid-rich foods are also rich in other nutrients and phytochemicals.

The same problem exists when researchers study the influence of flavonoids on heart disease. Results from some studies suggest protective effects, but no one is sure which nutrients are responsible. Scientists also do not know whether flavonoid supplements would have the same effects as eating flavonoid-rich foods.

FIGURING OUT THE BENEFITS OF PHYTOCHEMICALS

Even in the laboratory, understanding phytochemicals and how they prevent disease is complex. For example, apples, especially in their skins, are particularly rich in flavonoids and phenolics. Several studies have linked apple consumption to reduced risks of diseases, including cancer, asthma, diabetes, and heart disease. In lab petri dishes, apple skin phytochemicals inhibit the growth of liver cancer cells and colon cancer cells. In lab rats, the phytochemicals lower harmful cholesterol levels and lipids in their blood. They have been shown to protect against cholera, an infectious disease, but only in lab petri dishes.

Apple phytochemicals seem to have both antioxidant and anticancer actions, and these effects are not linked to the vitamins or fiber in the apples. However, complicating the picture is that varieties of apples have different levels of phytochemicals. For example, a Rome Beauty or Red Delicious has many more flavonoids and phenolics than a Cortland or Empire. Apples grown in partial shade have fewer phytochemicals than those exposed to full sun. Apple juice has only 10% of the antioxidant phytochemicals that fresh apples have.

Most nutrition scientists feel certain that phytochemicals are critical to the prevention of many diseases, but much more research is necessary before these chemicals are fully understood. Experts may feel confident about telling everyone to eat plenty of fruits and vegetables, or to be sure to eat the apple skin and the thin white membrane on an orange (both are particularly rich in phytochemicals). However, they cannot yet recommend supplemental doses or identify the phytochemicals associated with preventing a specific disease. As with essential nutrients, teasing apart the complex relationship between phytochemicals and disease is a continually evolving process.

REVIEW

Modern research is working out the complex relationship between nutrients and disease at a rapid pace, but how and why nutrition reduces the risk of disease is still an emerging science. Although much remains to be learned, nutritionists and medical professionals are already beginning to make nutritional recommendations based on the latest scientific studies. Some of the most exciting, substantial evidence of nutritionally based disease prevention involves vitamin D. Active vitamin D is manufactured by the body from sun exposure and UVB radiation, but scientists have determined that most people are deficient in this vitamin. Thousands of studies demonstrate an increased risk of disease in people with low levels of vitamin D in their blood. Most vitamin D scientists now recommend supplements for almost everyone. Another area of emerging nutritional research involves phytochemicals: chemicals in plants that are not essential to human life, but apparently critical to the prevention of disease. Many studies suggest that phytochemical-rich diets decrease the risk of cancer, heart disease, and other chronic diseases. Reliable evidence that specific phytochemicals protect against particular diseases is not yet available. Research is ongoing.

MAKING
NUTRITION DECISIONS

The science of nutrition turns out to be so complex that it can seem impossible to determine the best diet to prevent disease. New studies touting the importance of this or that nutrient seem to be reported almost daily in the media. Self-styled experts advocate different, sometimes extreme, approaches to nutrition and diet, perhaps in books or on the Internet. Making intelligent food choices means not only appreciating the relationship between nutrition and health, but also interpreting and analyzing the flow of information. While many new discoveries no doubt lie in the future, the evidence for the role of nutrition in preventing disease is substantial and strong. The building blocks of a healthy diet are well established. Ultimately, each individual is responsible for recognizing the essential role that nutrition plays in protecting lifelong health and deciding to care about the nutrients his or her body needs.

VARIED AND NATURAL

The American Dietetic Association (ADA) has good reason to recommend a widely varied diet. In ADA's *Complete Food and Nutrition Guide*, registered dietician Roberta Larson Duyff writes, "Why variety? Different food groups—and the nutrients and other substances their foods provide—help keep you healthy in different ways. No one nutrient, food, or food group has all you need, and none works alone." If recent nutritional research has demonstrated anything, it has demonstrated the proof of that assertion. As with apples, natural foods contain hundreds of protective, healthy substances that science is just beginning to explore. Some of these substances are well defined. Some are newly discovered and not completely understood. Many are still unknown. Eat the apple, however, and you get all the benefits, whether science understands them yet or not.

People probably need to eat diets similar to those of their ancestors to protect against cancer, heart disease, diabetes, and obesity. Civilization may have evolved, but our bodies have not changed since our hunter-gatherer days. We evolved to function optimally on a varied, flexible diet, and our bodies have come to depend upon the complex interaction of the chemical substances from natural foods. This means lean meats and other proteins, fruits, vegetables, nuts, seeds, and whole grains. Because we are not as active as our ancestors and do not face periodic starvation, we need to limit the fat in our diets and avoid "feasting" on high-calorie foods. Illnesses that plague modern humans may be prevented, in large part, by rejecting unnatural diets and choosing those that sustain health.

FUNCTIONAL FOODS

Natural fruits and vegetables are available in abundance, but few modern people have access to (or a desire for) wild roots and plants, mammoth haunches, or snails and grubs from the forest. Instead, we have fortified, enriched, or enhanced foods. This helps us to maintain a varied diet, along with the natural foods we consume. The ADA defines functional foods as whole foods and fortified foods that provide health benefits that may reduce disease risk. In 2009, the ADA released a position statement advocating functional foods when the benefits are scientifically substantiated. Examples of whole foods that decrease the risk of disease are broccoli, tomatoes, and nuts. Examples of enhanced foods are orange juice with added calcium, lutein-enriched eggs, and breads fortified with folic acid. As nutritional science progresses, more fortified foods are likely to become available, but the ADA warns that these foods alone cannot support health. A varied diet still is necessary.

MYPYRAMID

To help people choose a varied diet, the United States Department of Agriculture (USDA) developed MyPyramid, an interactive nutrition tool that describes the food groups and recommended proportions of foods needed for a healthy diet. The six food groups are grains, vegetables, fruits, oils, milk, and meat and beans. The six bands of the pyramid represent the varying recommended portions; there is a small band for oils and a large one for grains. Within each band, many food options are suggested. Vegetarians and vegans, for instance, can follow the MyPyramid recommendations by substituting other calcium sources for the milk group and other complete proteins in the meat and beans group. The MyPyramid plan even provides for "discretionary calories," to allow for some junk foods or sweet desserts. (See the Appendices for the MyPyramid chart.)

Almost everyone wants to eat for health and to prevent disease, but changing diet habits can be difficult. To people who have eaten white bread all their lives, whole-wheat bread may taste strange at first. Fast foods are cheap, filling, and tasty. Sugar cravings are better satisfied with a candy bar than with an apple. Microwavable, pre-made, high-fat sandwiches are easier to prepare than a balanced dinner of baked chicken, sweet potato, and spinach. Many people just are not used to natural, healthy foods and often do not like them.

LEARNING NEW FOOD HABITS

Limited diets lead to ill health. Diets deficient in any area described by MyPyramid are limited diets, no matter how many calories are consumed. Improving food habits is probably done best one step at a time, as Dr. Stice advocates with his Healthy Weight program to prevent obesity. In a document written for this program, Stice and his team outline four principles to help people improve dietary intake. The first principle is *substitution*. This means choosing healthier alternatives: mustard over mayonnaise, frozen yogurt instead of ice cream, pretzels rather than potato chips, fruit in place of candy. The program encourages individual decisions, so leaders ask each participant to identify one food they eat that they believe is the worst for them. Then, each person thinks of a healthy substitute. Each makes a commitment to substituting for the unhealthy food as often as possible. Eventually, explains Stice, the cravings for the unhealthy food fade and the healthy food is enjoyed.

Stice's second principle is *start your meal right*. Begin a meal with fruits, vegetables, soups, or salad. People who do this become full faster and are less likely to overeat unhealthy foods. The third principle is *smaller portion sizes*. This is especially helpful for people who are overweight or who eat too many high-fat foods. Everyone craves high-fat foods sometimes. The trick is not to feel deprived, but to limit yourself. For example, program leaders suggest eating ice cream out of a coffee cup (not a mug!) instead of a bowl, or never "super-sizing" a fast-food meal. Included in this principle is the recommendation to eat a meal of less variety. At first glance, this recommendation appears contradictory to healthful eating, but it is not. This principle means cutting out the least healthy parts of a meal. For instance, it means having either

FIGURE 9.1 In his popular 2004 documentary *Super Size Me*, director Morgan Spurlock discovered firsthand the consequences of a fast food diet by eating nothing but McDonald's for an entire month—and watching his health decline.

bread or potatoes, not both, at a single meal. Stice warns that it is best to NOT cut out vegetables or fruits.

The fourth and last principle is a *healthier food environment*. This means filling the kitchen and pantry with healthy foods, and not having unhealthy foods available. He also recommends avoiding environments with vending machines or snack shops. For example, a person may have to choose a different route home from school to avoid the doughnut shop. Another person might leave home with no money, so he or she cannot buy snacks.

Step by step, people following Stice's program learn to enjoy a healthy diet as a permanent lifestyle. Motivation comes from exercises, such as making a list of the top 10 reasons for changing food habits, or keeping a food record for a few days. The program also recommends that people continually try new healthy foods, note and appreciate successes, and reward themselves for eating healthier with a fun activity. The program recognizes that the path to a healthy diet is not always smooth. Stice says, "Stay committed to a healthy lifestyle and realize that sometimes you will slip—but the important thing is to view these slips as opportunities to learn how to <u>not</u> slip next time. If you view it as a lifelong process, you can see that one slip-up is not complete failure."

TO SUPPLEMENT OR NOT TO SUPPLEMENT?

Some experts recommend supplements for people who do not get complete, balanced nutrition from their diets. Dyuff, for example, suggests that anyone unable or unwilling to eat a healthy diet may need a good multivitamin and mineral supplement. However, no one should depend upon supplements to fulfill all of their nutritional needs. Dyuff explains in the *Complete Food and Nutrition Guide*, "Only food can provide the mixture of vitamins, minerals, phytonutrients, and other substances for health—qualities that can't be duplicated with dietary supplements alone."

Choosing a healthy, varied diet over supplements is standard mainstream nutritional advice, but some experts disagree. For example, Dr. Michael F. Roizen and Dr. Mehmet C. Oz, in their book *You: The Owner's Manual*, recommend a daily multivitamin and mineral supplement for everyone, no matter his or her diet. Some experts recommend supplements of folic acid for all women of childbearing age. This is because by the time a woman knows she is pregnant, it may be too late to correct any folic acid insufficiency that may cause neural tube defects in the developing fetus. The Linus Pauling Institute at Oregon State University recommends a daily multivitamin and mineral supplement, as well as a vitamin D supplement (2,000 IU), a vitamin E supplement (200 IU), and a calcium supplement when foods do not supply at

FIGURE 9.2 Some nutrition experts recommend that people who do not get complete and balanced nutrition from their diet may take supplements. Generally, though, most experts note that supplements are not replacements for a healthy, varied diet.

least 1,000 mg of calcium. In some cases, the Institute also recommends extra vitamin C. At the same time, the Institute lists food recommendations that include a minimum of two cups each of fruits and vegetables daily, fish twice a week, nuts, seeds, olive oil, and the replacement of "white foods" such as bread and potatoes with whole grains. In general, most nutritional experts note that supplements are not replacements for a healthy, varied diet.

SUPER FOODS

Instead of adding pills to the diet, some nutrition experts suggest supplementing your diet with "super foods" as the way to ensure good health. In an article for WebMD, public health expert Kathleen M. Zelman lists 10 foods with multiple disease-fighting nutrients. They provide the nutrients that Zelman and other

PROBIOTICS

Probiotics are live microorganisms—usually bacteria—that have beneficial effects in the human body. Some people depend upon probiotic foods or supplements to maintain nutritional health and prevent diseases. Beneficial bacteria exist by the millions in the human digestive system. They help to protect against harmful bacteria, strengthen the immune system, and help to absorb and digest nutrients. These so-called "friendly" bacteria can be killed when people take antibiotics or when an infection from invading bacteria overwhelms them. The friendly bacteria can be replaced with probiotic foods, such as yogurt, fermented milk, tempeh, miso, and some soy drinks. Yeast is a source of probiotic microorganisms, too. Scientists say that probiotic foods may help treat diarrhea, urinary tract infections, yeast infections, and childhood eczema (a skin condition). Research is ongoing about whether probiotics can help decrease the risk of bladder cancer or whether nutritionists say are often missing in the average American diet. The 10 foods are yogurt, eggs, nuts, kiwi fruit, quinoa (a whole grain), beans, salmon, broccoli, sweet potatoes, and berries. These foods provide the macronutrients, micronutrients, antioxidants, and phytochemicals that may best prevent disease.

People have different ideas about super foods. Dr. Nicholas Perricone, a dermatologist and nutrition writer, has his own list. His includes wild salmon, allium (onions, garlic, leeks, and chives), oatmeal, blueberries, ginger root, virgin olive oil, nuts and seeds, brightly colored fruits and vegetables, sprouts, and yogurt. Other nutrition advisors list super foods that are specific to heart health, losing weight, anti-aging, improving brain power, fighting cancer, building muscles, and even getting a good night's sleep. For example, Oprah Winfrey recommends the acai berry from Brazil as her top super food. Doctors Per-

they can prevent harmful bacteria from getting through mucous membranes and attacking the body. Scientists are wary about some probiotic health claims, however. The claims made by some manufacturers of probiotic supplements have not been scientifically tested. Few scientific studies provide evidence that these supplements improve overall health or that the bacteria themselves even remain alive and healthy in capsules or pills. In some cases, products advertised as rich in probiotics actually contain little to none. In others, the microorganisms are not the same as the ones needed by human bodies. In addition, no studies have proved that probiotics can "cleanse" or "detoxify" the body. While probiotics are, by definition, not harmful, people may have allergic reactions to the supplements. The long-term effects of taking the supplements also are unknown. In general, scientists recommend getting probiotics from foods.

ricone and Oz believe that the acai berry can improve energy, fight aging, normalize digestion, remove toxins from the body, and prevent disease.

Extracts of acai berry have been sold by some companies as diet pills and weight-loss supplements. However, scientists and researchers question these claims. Acai berries are rich in anti-oxidants and phytochemicals, but few scientific studies have been done on the berry's effects in the body. A small study published in 2008 showed that the antioxidants in acai berries could be absorbed and metabolized by people, but it is still unknown if there are disease-prevention benefits or what quantity is ideal. The Center for Science in the Public Interest, a scientific advocacy organization, says there is no evidence that acai berries have weight-loss properties. Acai berries are at least as healthy as other berries, perhaps moreso, but they are not a magic food.

MAKE CHOICES BASED ON SCIENCE, NOT HYPE

Some nutritional recommendations are backed by science, but many are not. Although it is always a good idea to eat a varied diet that is rich in nutrients and phytochemicals, no one food or short list of foods can perform health miracles. It can be hard to know which advice to follow. In addition, while no natural food can do any harm (assuming the person is not allergic or sensitive to it), some herbal concoctions and supplements that are touted as super foods or miracle cures can be toxic. The ADA recommends that everyone learn the difference between science-based nutrition information and preliminary studies or outright misinformation. According to the ADA, the media often exaggerate the meaning of single scientific studies. Also, says the ADA, unscrupulous individuals may engage in food "quackery" for financial gain. The ADA Web site, EatRight.org, lists six ways to be a smart consumer of nutrition information. People can:

- Question the qualifications of authors, presenters, and other nutrition advocates, as well as the evidence for any claims or advice.
- Take steps to evaluate nutrition reports or promotions before they become victims of the ploys, by becoming more aware of the many ways misinformation, food fraud, and quackery are conveyed.
- Think critically about food and nutrition messages used to promote the sale of products or services.
- Ask a qualified nutrition expert for help in evaluating a statement, product, or service.
- Inquire at the medical or nutrition department of a nearby university or college, or at the food and nutrition department of a local hospital/medical center, to obtain current and accurate information and to find nutrition services for the public.
- Check with the American Dietetic Association if they have questions or concerns.

EVALUATE EVIDENCE CAREFULLY

One of the best ways to evaluate nutritional information is to ask whether it is based on scientific evidence. Testimonials from people who say their diseases were cured by a specific nutrient or supplement are not good evidence that a claim is real. Anecdotes, or stories, of people who were healed by certain foods are not scientific, either. This kind of reporting omits all the people who were not helped by the nutrients. The sample size, or number of people who tried this cure, is almost always very small. Even a few hundred reports may not reflect what would happen for most people.

Nutritional claims for disease prevention are not supported by correlation. This means that just because two things occur together does not prove that one caused the other. For example, scientists know that obesity and type 2 diabetes often occur together, but they are still not certain that obesity causes diabetes, although it is known to be a risk factor. Perhaps, in some people, the same genes that cause obesity also cause diabetes. Or perhaps a third factor—such as stress or a low birth weight—is the underlying cause of both. Or perhaps certain foods that cause diabetes also cause obesity. Correlation does not prove causation, and that is why scientists are so careful about making claims for different phytochemicals or antioxidants for disease prevention. When hundreds of phytochemicals exists in the same food, it takes careful experimentation to identify the substances that are meaningful.

A single study or experiment may be interesting, but it cannot be used to make nutrition decisions. Other scientists have to evaluate the study and repeat it to see if they get the same results.

HEALTHY AND HARMFUL HERBALS

Herbs are plants that are usually not eaten as foods, but are considered valuable for their flavors, scents, or nutritional or medicinal properties. The effectiveness of herbal supplements for maintaining health and preventing disease may or may not be backed by scientific evidence. And some herbal supplements can be dangerous. Echinacea, for example, is a flowering plant. Some scientific studies support the claim that it can prevent and treat the common cold, while others do not show a benefit. Several studies provide evidence that green tea extracts act as antioxidants and may reduce cancer risk. Use of other herbal supplements is supported by some preliminary scientific evidence, although more research is needed. These include ginger for nausea, garlic to improve immune system functioning and reduce cholesterol and high blood pressure, and St. John's wort to ease symptoms of depression.

What happens in a laboratory petri dish may not happen in a group of laboratory rats, and what cures rats may not help people. Until results have been confirmed many times and under many conditions, the importance of a nutrient dosage is not known for sure. Nutrition professionals suggest using caution and intelligence when evaluating any claims about nutrients and the prevention of disease. Despite the rapid pace of nutritional investigation, confirmation comes slowly because no reputable researchers want to draw premature conclusions or offer inaccurate advice.

When it comes to human nutrition and the prevention of disease, many complex interactions are involved. Scientists have few quick fixes. They do know, however, that nutrition is critical to the prevention of many more diseases than people suspected in the past. They look forward to a future when nutritional intervention is a key part of the treatment plans and cures for many diseases.

Scientific studies find no value to claims that ginseng can control diabetes, improve exercise ability, or improve sexual performance. Studies also do not support that ginkgo biloba prevents altitude sickness. Ma huang (ephedra) has been shown to be dangerous and banned as a supplement in the United States. It has been associated with strokes, heart attacks, and deaths. Another dangerous herbal supplement is called Yohimbine. This substance is said to increase muscle mass and help with weight loss. However, it can seriously affect heart rhythms and blood pressure.

Herbal supplements may be "natural," but that does not mean they are harmless. About 30% of modern drugs are made from plants, and any drug has the potential to be both powerful and toxic, especially in large amounts. The toxic effects of many herbal substances have not yet been determined.

Until that day comes, we can all choose to eat the most varied, natural diets possible, so as to give ourselves the best chance to get all the nutrients we may need to live long and healthy lives.

REVIEW

Choosing the best diet to prevent disease can seem difficult, but the general principles for healthy eating are well established. The American Dietetic Association explains that a varied diet, dependent upon no one food or food group, is best. Fortified or enhanced foods can be part of a healthy, varied diet, along with whole, natural foods. Following the USDA's MyPyramid is likely to optimize nutritional intake, but developing new food habits and retraining likes and dislikes may be necessary. Some authorities recommend vitamin and mineral supplements to ensure an adequate nutrient intake. Others recommend "super foods" along with or instead of supplements. However, no super food, not even the richest in nutrients, is a miracle food or a magic cure. People need to evaluate nutritional claims and assure themselves that these claims are based upon sound science. Much more remains to be learned about the connection between nutrition and disease prevention, but people can use current knowledge to give themselves the best chance for long, healthy life.

APPENDIX A

DIETARY REFERENCE INTAKES

ACCEPTABLE MACRONUTRIENT DISTRIBUTION RANGES (AMDR) FOR HEALTHY DIETS AS A PERCENTAGE OF ENERGY						
Age	Carbohydrates	Added Sugars	Total Fat	Linoleic Acid	α-Linolenic Acid	Protein
1–3 years old	45–65	25	30–40	5–10	0.6–1.2	5–20
4–18 years old	45–65	25	25–35	5–10	0.6–1.2	10–30
≥ 19 years old	45–65	25	20–35	5–10	0.6–1.2	10–35

Source: Institute of Medicine, Food and Nutrition Board. "Dietary Reference Intakes for Energy, Carbohydrates, Fiber, Fat, Protein, and Amino Acids." Washington, D.C.: National Academies Press, 2002.

RECOMMENDED INTAKES OF VITAMINS FOR VARIOUS AGE GROUPS

Life Stage	Vit A (µg/day)	Vit C (mg/day)	Vit D (µg/day)	Vit E (mg/day)	Vit K (mg/day)
Infants					
0–6 mo	400	40	5	4	2.0
7–12 mo	500	50	5	5	2.5
Children					
1–3 yrs	**300**	**15**	5	**6**	30
4–8 yrs	**400**	**25**	5	**7**	55
Males					
9–13 yrs	**600**	**45**	5	**11**	60
14–18 yrs	**900**	**75**	5	**15**	75
19–30 yrs	**900**	**90**	5	**15**	120
31–50 yrs	**900**	**90**	5	**15**	120
51–70 yrs	**900**	**90**	10	**15**	120
70 yrs	**900**	**90**	15	**15**	120
Females					
9–13 yrs	**600**	**45**	5	**11**	60
14–18 yrs	**700**	**65**	5	**15**	75
19–30 yrs	**700**	**75**	5	**15**	90
31–50 yrs	**700**	**75**	5	**15**	90
51–70 yrs	**700**	**75**	10	**15**	90
70 yrs	**700**	**75**	15	**15**	90
Pregnancy					
18 yrs	**750**	**80**	5	**15**	75
19–30 yrs	**770**	**85**	5	**15**	90
31–50 yrs	**770**	**85**	5	**15**	90
Lactation					
18 yrs	**1,200**	**115**	5	**19**	75
19–30 yrs	**1,300**	**120**	5	**19**	90
31–50 yrs	**1,300**	**120**	5	**19**	90

RECOMMENDED INTAKES OF VITAMINS FOR VARIOUS AGE GROUPS

Life Stage	Thiamin (mg/day)	Riboflavin (mg/day)	Niacin (mg/day)	Vit B$_6$ (mg/day)	Folate (µg/day)
Infants					
0–6 mo	0.2	0.3	2	0.1	65
7–12 mo	0.3	0.4	4	0.3	80
Children					
1–3 yrs	**0.5**	**0.5**	**6**	**0.5**	**150**
4–8 yrs	**0.6**	**0.6**	**8**	**0.6**	**200**
Males					
9–13 yrs	**0.9**	**0.9**	**12**	**1.0**	**300**
14–18 yrs	**1.2**	**1.3**	**16**	**1.3**	**400**
19–30 yrs	**1.2**	**1.3**	**16**	**1.3**	**400**
31–50 yrs	**1.2**	**1.3**	**16**	**1.3**	**400**
51–70 yrs	**1.2**	**1.3**	**16**	**1.7**	**400**
70 yrs	**1.2**	**1.3**	**16**	**1.7**	**400**
Females					
9–13 yrs	**0.9**	**0.9**	**12**	**1.0**	**300**
14–18 yrs	**1.0**	**1.0**	**14**	**1.2**	**400**
19–30 yrs	**1.1**	**1.1**	**14**	**1.3**	**400**
31–50 yrs	**1.1**	**1.1**	**14**	**1.3**	**400**
51–70 yrs	**1.1**	**1.1**	**14**	**1.5**	**400**
70 yrs	**1.1**	**1.1**	**14**	**1.5**	**400**
Pregnancy					
18 yrs	**1.4**	**1.4**	**18**	**1.9**	**600**
19–30 yrs	**1.4**	**1.4**	**18**	**1.9**	**600**
31–50 yrs	**1.4**	**1.4**	**18**	**1.9**	**600**
Lactation					
18 yrs	**1.4**	**1.6**	**17**	**2.0**	**500**
19–30 yrs	**1.4**	**1.6**	**17**	**2.0**	**500**
31–50 yrs	**1.4**	**1.6**	**17**	**2.0**	**500**

(continues)

RECOMMENDED INTAKES OF VITAMINS FOR VARIOUS AGE GROUPS (continued)

Life Stage	Vit B$_{12}$ (µg/day)	Pantothenic Acid (mg/day)	Biotin Group (µg/day)	Choline* (mg/day)
Infants				
0–6 mo	0.4	1.7	5	125
7–12 mo	0.5	1.8	6	150
Children				
1–3 yrs	0.9	2	8	200
4–8 yrs	1.2	3	12	250
Males				
9–13 yrs	1.8	4	20	375
14–18 yrs	2.4	5	25	550
19–30 yrs	2.4	5	30	550
31–50 yrs	2.4	5	30	550
51–70 yrs	2.4	5	30	550
70 yrs	2.4	5	30	550
Females				
9–13 yrs	1.8	4	20	375
14–18 yrs	2.4	5	25	400
19–30 yrs	2.4	5	30	425
31–50 yrs	2.4	5	30	425
51–70 yrs	2.4	5	30	425
70 yrs	2.4	5	30	425
Pregnancy				
18 yrs	2.6	6	30	450
19–30 yrs	2.6	6	30	450
31–50 yrs	2.6	6	30	450
Lactation				
18 yrs	2.8	7	35	550
19–30 yrs	2.8	7	35	550
31–50 yrs	2.8	7	35	550

Note: This table presents Recommended Dietary Allowances (RDAs) in bold type and Adequate Intakes (AIs) in ordinary type.

* Not yet classified as a vitamin

Source: Adapted from Dietary Reference Intake Tables: The Complete Set. Institute of Medicine, National Academy of Sciences. Available online at www.nap.edu.

RECOMMENDED INTAKES OF SELECTED MINERALS FOR VARIOUS AGE GROUPS

	Calcium (mg/day)	Chromium (µg/day)	Copper (µg/day)	Fluroide (mg/day)	Iodine (µg/day)
Infants					
0–6 mo	210	0.2	200	0.01	110
7–12 mo	270	5.5	220	0.5	130
Children					
1–3 yrs	500	11	**340**	0.7	**90**
4–8 yrs	800	15	**440**	1	**90**
Males					
9–13 yrs	1,300	25	**700**	2	**120**
14–18 yrs	1,300	35	**890**	3	**150**
19–30 yrs	1,000	35	**900**	4	**150**
31–50 yrs	1,000	35	**900**	4	**150**
51–70 yrs	1,200	30	**900**	4	**150**
70 yrs	1,200	30	**900**	4	**150**
Females					
9–13 yrs	1,300	21	**700**	2	**120**
14–18 yrs	1,300	24	**890**	3	**150**
19–30 yrs	1,000	25	**900**	3	**150**
31–50 yrs	1,000	25	**900**	3	**150**
51–70 yrs	1,200	20	**900**	3	**150**
70 yrs	1,200	20	**900**	3	**150**
Pregnancy					
18 yrs	1,300	29	**1,000**	3	**220**
19–30 yrs	1,000	30	**1,000**	3	**220**
31–50 yrs	1,000	30	**1,000**	3	**220**
Lactation					
18 yrs	1,300	44	**1,300**	3	**290**
19–30 yrs	1,000	45	**1,300**	3	**290**
31–50 yrs	1,000	45	**1,300**	3	**290**

(continues)

RECOMMENDED INTAKES OF SELECTED MINERALS FOR VARIOUS AGE GROUPS (continued)				
	Iron (mg/day)	Magnesium (mg/day)	Phosphorus (mg/day)	Selenium (µg/day)
Infants				
0–6 mo	0.27	30	100	15
7–12 mo	11	75	275	20
Children				
1–3 yrs	7	80	460	20
4–8 yrs	10	130	500	30
Males				
9–13 yrs	8	240	1,250	40
14–18 yrs	11	410	1,250	55
19–30 yrs	8	400	700	55
31–50 yrs	8	420	700	55
51–70 yrs	8	420	700	55
70 yrs	8	420	700	55
Females				
9–13 yrs	8	240	1,250	40
14–18 yrs	15	360	1,250	55
19–30 yrs	18	310	700	55
31–50 yrs	18	320	700	55
51–70 yrs	8	320	700	55
70 yrs	8	320	700	55
Pregnancy				
18 yrs	27	400	1,250	60
19–30 yrs	27	350	700	60
31–50 yrs	27	360	700	60
Lactation				
18 yrs	10	360	1,250	70
19–30 yrs	9	310	700	70
31–50 yrs	9	320	700	70

RECOMMENDED INTAKES OF SELECTED MINERALS FOR VARIOUS AGE GROUPS

	Zinc (mg/day)	Sodium (g/day)	Chloride (g/day)	Potassium (g/day)
Infants				
0–6 mo	2	0.12	0.18	0.4
7–12 mo	**3**	0.37	0.57	0.7
Children				
1–3 yrs	**3**	1.0	1.5	3.0
4–8 yrs	**5**	1.2	1.9	3.8
Males				
9–13 yrs	**8**	1.5	2.3	4.5
14–18 yrs	**11**	1.5	2.3	4.7
19–30 yrs	**11**	1.5	2.3	4.7
31–50 yrs	**11**	1.5	2.3	4.7
51–70 yrs	**11**	1.3	2.0	4.7
70 yrs	**11**	1.2	1.8	4.7
Females				
9–13 yrs	**8**	1.5	2.3	4.5
14–18 yrs	**9**	1.5	2.3	4.7
19–30 yrs	**8**	1.5	2.3	4.7
31–50 yrs	**8**	1.5	2.3	4.7
51–70 yrs	**8**	1.3	2.0	4.7
70 yrs	**8**	1.2	1.8	4.7
Pregnancy				
18 yrs	**13**	1.5	2.3	4.7
19–30 yrs	**11**	1.5	2.3	4.7
31–50 yrs	**11**	1.5	2.3	4.7
Lactation				
18 yrs	**14**	1.5	2.3	5.1
19–30 yrs	**12**	1.5	2.3	5.1
31–50 yrs	**12**	1.5	2.3	5.1

Note: This table presents Recommended Dietary Allowances (RDAs) in bold type and Adequate Intakes (AIs) in ordinary type.

Source: Adapted from Dietary Reference Intake Tables: The Complete Set. *Institute of Medicine, National Academy of Sciences. Available online at www.nap.edu.*

APPENDIX B

HEALTHY BODY WEIGHTS
Body Mass Index (BMI)

Body mass index, or BMI, is the measurement of choice for determining health risks associated with body weight. BMI uses a mathematical formula that takes into account both a person's height and weight. BMI equals a person's weight in kilograms divided by height in meters squared (BMI=kg/m^2).

RISK OF ASSOCIATED DISEASE ACCORDING TO BMI AND WAIST SIZE FOR ADULTS			
BMI		Waist less than or equal to 40 in. (men) or 35 in. (women)	Waist greater than 40 in. (men) or 35 in. (women)
18.5 or less	Underweight	--	N/A
18.5–24.9	Normal	--	N/A
25.0–29.9	Overweight	Increased	High
30.0–34.9	Obese	High	Very High
35.0–39.9	Obese	Very High	Very High
40 or greater	Extremely Obese	Extremely High	Extremely High

Determining Your Body Mass Index (BMI)

To use the table on the following page, find the appropriate height in the left-hand column. Move across the row to the given weight. The number at the top of the column is the BMI for that height and weight. Then use the table above to determine how at risk you are for developing a weight-related disease.

BMI (kg/m²)	19	20	21	22	23	24	25	26	27	28	29	30	35	40
Height (in.)							Weight (lb)							
58	91	96	100	105	110	115	119	124	129	134	138	143	167	191
59	94	99	104	109	114	119	124	128	133	138	143	148	173	198
60	97	102	107	112	118	123	128	133	138	143	148	153	179	204
61	100	106	111	116	122	127	132	137	143	148	153	158	185	211
62	104	109	115	120	126	131	136	142	147	153	158	164	191	218
63	107	113	118	124	130	135	141	146	152	158	163	169	197	225
64	110	116	122	128	134	140	145	151	157	163	169	174	204	232
65	114	120	126	132	138	144	150	156	162	168	174	180	210	240
66	118	124	130	136	142	148	155	161	167	173	179	186	216	247
67	121	127	134	140	146	153	159	166	172	178	185	191	223	255
68	125	131	138	144	151	158	164	171	177	184	190	197	230	262
69	128	135	142	149	155	162	169	176	182	189	196	203	236	270
70	132	139	146	153	160	167	174	181	188	195	202	207	243	278
71	136	143	150	157	165	172	179	186	193	200	208	215	250	286
72	140	147	154	162	169	177	184	191	199	206	213	221	258	294
73	144	151	159	166	174	182	189	197	204	212	219	227	265	302
74	148	155	163	171	179	186	194	202	210	218	225	233	272	311
75	152	160	168	176	184	192	200	208	216	224	232	240	279	319
76	156	164	172	180	189	197	205	213	221	230	238	246	287	328

Source: Adapted from Partnership for Healthy Weight Management, http://www.consumer.gov/weightloss/bmi.htm.

BMI-FOR-AGE GROWTH CHARTS

2 to 20 years: Boys
Body mass index-for-age percentiles

NAME _____

RECORD # _____

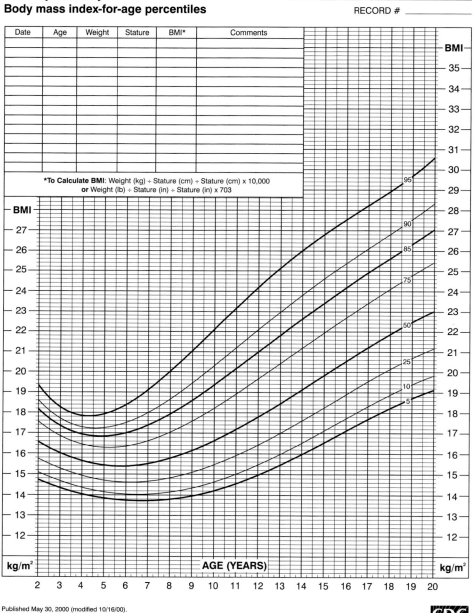

*To Calculate BMI: Weight (kg) ÷ Stature (cm) ÷ Stature (cm) x 10,000
or Weight (lb) ÷ Stature (in) ÷ Stature (in) x 703

AGE (YEARS)

Published May 30, 2000 (modified 10/16/00).
SOURCE: Developed by the National Center for Health Statistics in collaboration with
the National Center for Chronic Disease Prevention and Health Promotion (2000).
http://www.cdc.gov/growthcharts

SAFER · HEALTHIER · PEOPLE™

2 to 20 years: Girls
Body mass index-for-age percentiles

NAME _____

RECORD # _____

Date	Age	Weight	Stature	BMI*	Comments

*To Calculate BMI: Weight (kg) ÷ Stature (cm) ÷ Stature (cm) x 10,000
or Weight (lb) ÷ Stature (in) ÷ Stature (in) x 703

BMI 35, 34, 33, 32, 31, 30, 29, 28, 27, 26, 25, 24, 23, 22, 21, 20, 19, 18, 17, 16, 15, 14, 13, 12

95, 90, 85, 75, 50, 25, 10, 5

kg/m² — AGE (YEARS) — kg/m²

2 3 4 5 6 7 8 9 10 11 12 13 14 15 16 17 18 19 20

Published May 30, 2000 (modified 10/16/00).
SOURCE: Developed by the National Center for Health Statistics in collaboration with
the National Center for Chronic Disease Prevention and Health Promotion (2000).
http://www.cdc.gov/growthcharts

CDC
SAFER · HEALTHIER · PEOPLE™

APPENDIX C

BLOOD VALUES OF NUTRITIONAL RELEVANCE

Red blood cells	
Men	4.6–6.2 million/mm^3
Women	4.2–5.2 million/mm^3
White blood cells	5,000–10,000/mm^3
Calcium	9–11 mg/100 mL
Iron	
Men	75–175 µg/100 mL
Women	65–165 µg/100 mL
Zinc	0.75–1.4 µg/mL
Potassium	3.5–5.0 mEq/L
Sodium	136–145 mEq/L
Vitamin A	20–80 µg/100 mL
Vitamin B$_{12}$	200–800 pg/100 mL
Vitamin C	0.6–2.0 mg/100 mL
Folate	2–20 ng/mL
pH	7.35–7.45
Total protein	6.6–8.0 g/100 mL
Albumin	3.0–4.0 g/100 mL
Cholesterol	less than 200 mg/100 mL
Glucose	60–100 mg/100 mL blood, 70–120 mg/100 mL serum

Source: Handbook of Clinical Dietetics, *American Dietetic Association (New Haven, Conn.: Yale University Press, 1981); and Committee on Dietetics of the Mayo Clinic,* Mayo Clinic Diet Manual *(Philadelphia: W. B. Saunders Company, 1981), pp. 275–277.*

APPENDIX D

USDA'S MYPYRAMID

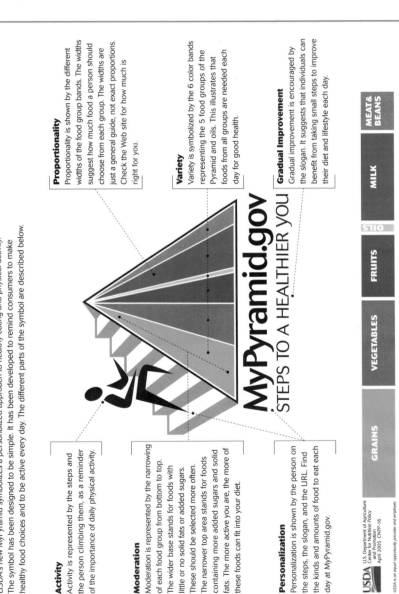

Anatomy of MyPyramid

One size doesn't fit all

USDA's new MyPyramid symbolizes a personalized approach to healthy eating and physical activity. The symbol has been designed to be simple. It has been developed to remind consumers to make healthy food choices and to be active every day. The different parts of the symbol are described below.

Activity

Activity is represented by the steps and the person climbing them, as a reminder of the importance of daily physical activity.

Moderation

Moderation is represented by the narrowing of each food group from bottom to top. The wider base stands for foods with little or no solid fats or added sugars. These should be selected more often. The narrower top area stands for foods containing more added sugars and solid fats. The more active you are, the more of these foods can fit into your diet.

Personalization

Personalization is shown by the person on the steps, the slogan, and the URL. Find the kinds and amounts of food to eat each day at MyPyramid.gov.

Proportionality

Proportionality is shown by the different widths of the food group bands. The widths suggest how much food a person should choose from each group. The widths are just a general guide, not exact proportions. Check the Web site for how much is right for you.

Variety

Variety is symbolized by the 6 color bands representing the 5 food groups of the Pyramid and oils. This illustrates that foods from all groups are needed each day for good health.

Gradual Improvement

Gradual improvement is encouraged by the slogan. It suggests that individuals can benefit from taking small steps to improve their diet and lifestyle each day.

MyPyramid.gov
STEPS TO A HEALTHIER YOU

GRAINS   VEGETABLES   FRUITS   OILS   MILK   MEAT & BEANS

U.S. Department of Agriculture
Center for Nutrition Policy and Promotion
April 2005 CNPP-16

USDA is an equal opportunity provider and employer.

Source: http://www.mypyramid.gov/downloads/MyPyramid_Anatomy.pdf.

GLOSSARY

Allele   Either of a pair of alternative forms of a gene

Amino acids   The building blocks of proteins; molecules of these chemical substances are joined together in chains of varying proportions to form proteins.

Anabolism   The phase of metabolism in which simple substances are built into complex substances, such as living tissue.

Antibody   A specialized immune system protein produced in response to a foreign substance; antibodies are made by white blood cells and circulate in the bloodstream, where they act as the body's army in order to detect and destroy invaders such as bacteria.

Antioxidants   Substances that prevent oxidation and the damage caused to cells by free radicals; vitamin C, vitamin E, vitamin A, and zinc are examples of nutrient antioxidants.

Apoptosis   Programmed cell death; it is a form of cellular suicide in the presence of sufficient cell damage.

Autoimmune disease   A disease in which the immune system mistakenly launches an attack against its own tissues as if it is a foreign invader

Calories   A measure of the energy released by food; calories in the diet are actually kilocalories—1,000 of the heat units required to raise the temperature of a gram of water in the laboratory by a specific amount. Calories in food are also called "nutritionist's calories."

Catabolism   The phase of metabolism in which complex substances are broken down into simple substances resulting in the release of energy

Cholecalciferol   Vitamin D3; the kind of vitamin D made by the body when sunlight is absorbed by the skin

Correlated   Occurring with, but not necessarily causal

Electrolytes   The salts and minerals that conduct electrical impulses in the body, such as sodium chloride (table salt), potassium, and calcium; they control the fluid balance in the body. Therefore, electrolyte balance is critical to normal body functioning.

Enzymes   Protein molecules that act as catalysts, aiding and speeding chemical reactions and metabolism

Ergocalciferol   Vitamin D2; this form of vitamin D comes from plants and some fungi exposed to ultraviolet light, but does not occur naturally in the human body.

Fat soluable   Capable of being dissolved in fats and oils; fat soluable vitamins include vitamin A, vitamin D, and vitamin K.

Fatty acids   Molecules that form long chains in fats and oils in both plants and animals; essential fatty acids are substances produced by plants that cannot be made by the human body but are required for health. A polyunsaturated oil, such as safflower oil, is a good source of essential fatty acids.

Fortification   The addition of nutrients to foods, such as adding folic acid to bread or vitamin D to milk; it is sometimes called enrichment or enhancement.

Free radicals   Byproducts of cell functioning in which unstable atoms are released when oxygen interacts with cell molecules; free radicals are the result of oxidation and can cause a chain reaction of cell damage.

Gastrointestinal   Relating to the stomach and intestines

Gene expression   The translation of information in a gene into the protein or signal for which it codes

Genome   All of the genetic information—the entire DNA sequence—of an organism

Genotype   An individual's genetic makeup or specific combination of genes; genotype interacts with the environment to determine phenotype.

Glucose   A simple sugar that is the most important source of energy in the body and the main type of sugar in the blood; the body breaks down foods, especially carbohydrates, to produce glucose.

Hormones   Chemical substances produced by one part of the body to control, signal, or regulate other parts; estrogen and insulin are examples of hormones.

Immune system   The system that protects the body from foreign invaders, such as harmful bacteria, fungi, and viruses; several kinds of white blood cells and protective barriers, such as mucous membranes are components of the immune system.

Inborn error of metabolism (IEM)   A genetic, inherited disease that results in a defect in a specific enzyme

Lipids   Fats stored in the body as energy reserves or used as components of cells; triglycerides and cholesterol are examples of lipids.

Macronutrients   Nutrients needed in large amounts, such as water, protein, carbohydrates, and fats

Metabolism   All the chemical processes involved in changing one substance (food, for example) into another so that it can be used by the body for survival, energy, maintenance, storage, growth, reproduction, and health

Micronutrients   Nutrients required in relatively small amounts for healthy body functioning; vitamins and most minerals are micronutrients.

Nutrient   Any substance that can be metabolized for energy, growth or health

Obese   Having a BMI of 30 or greater (in an adult)

Overweight   Having a BMI between 25 and 29.9 (in an adult)

Phenotype   All the observable characteristics of an organism; phenotype results from interactions between the genotype and the environment.

Phytochemicals   Protective chemical compounds produced by plants that are not nutrients or recognized as essential for humans but seem to have health-protective qualities; they are also known as phytonutrients.

Protein energy malnutrition (PEM)   A potentially fatal nutritional disorder in which there is a severe deficit in either energy (calories) or protein; the three main forms of PEM are marasmus, kwashiorkor, and marasmic kwashiorkor.

Substrate   The material upon which an enzyme acts

Water-soluble   Able to dissolve in water; water-soluble vitamins are easily absorbed by the body but not stored. The body uses what it needs and then excretes any excess in the urine. Examples include vitamin C and folic acid.

Zygote   The fertilized egg

BIBLIOGRAPHY

"About BMI for Children and Teens," Healthy Weight: Centers for Disease Control and Prevention (CDC). Available Online. URL: http://www.cdc.gov/healthyweight/assessing/bmi/childrens_BMI/about_childrens_BMI.html.

"Acute Malnutrition: A Highly Prevalent, Frequently Fatal, Imminently Treatable, Neglected Disease," Publications: International Activity Report 2006, Doctors without Borders. Available Online. URL: http://doctorswithoutborders.org/publications/ar/report.cfm?id=3228.

ADA's Public Relations Team, "What is an Antioxidant?" Eat Right. org, American Dietetic Association, September 14, 2006. Available Online. URL: http://www.eatright.org/cps/rde/xchg/ada/hs.xsl/home_9660_ENU_HTML.htm.

Ananias, Patrus. "Implementing the Human Right to Food in Brazil," 2008, reprinted at Hunger Notes, World Hunger.org. Available Online. URL: http://www.worldhunger.org/articles/08/hrf/ananias.htm.

Astley, Sian B. "Dietetics Today—Nutrigenomics Tomorrow?" Nutrigenomics Role—Expectations, NuGO: The European Nutrigenomics Organisation. Available Online. URL: http://www.nugo.org/everyone/34104/34076.

Balzer, Benjamin. "Introduction to the Paleolithic Diet," Earth360. Available Online. URL: http://www.earth360.com/diet_paleodiet_balzer.html.

Barrett, Stephen and Harriet Hall. "Dubious Genetic Testing," Quackwatch, 2002-2003 and Updated November 24, 2008. Available Online. URL: http://www.quackwatch.com/01QuackeryRelatedTopics/Tests/genomics.html.

"Body Worlds 2: Amazing Facts about the Human Body." Denver Museum of Nature & Science. Available Online. URL: http://www.

dmns.org/main/en/Professionals/Press/Press+Release+Archives/ Press+Releases/Exhibitions/bodyWorldsAmazingFacts.htm.

Bowron, Craig. "Vitamin D Nears Superstar Status, as Few Get Enough," Health, Minneapolis Post, October 22, 2009. Available Online. URL: http://www.minnpost.com/craigbowron/2008/10/22/4009/ vitamin_d_nears_superstar_status_as_few_get_enough.

Boyer, Jeanelle, and Rui Hai Liu. "Apple Phytochemicals and Their Health Benefits," *Nutrition Journal*, Vol. 3, No. 5, May 12, 2004, BioMed Central Ltd. Reprint. Available Online. URL: http://www. nutritionj.com/content/3/1/5.

Carter, J. Stein. "Complementary Protein and Diet," University of Cincinnati Clermont College, Biology Class Lecture. Available Online. URL: http://biology.clc.uc.edu/courses/bio104/compprot.htm.

Chimhete, Caiphas. "Zimbabwe: Prisoners Eat Rats as Death Toll rises," The Zimbabwe Standard, AllAfrica Global Media, May 16, 2009. Available Online. URL: http://allafrica.com/stories/200905181522. html.

Chous, A. Paul, MA, OD, FAAO. " 'D' is for Diabetes: Low Vitamin D Levels Linked to Increased Risk of Disease," dLife.com, June 30, 2009. Available Online. URL: http://www.dlife.com/dLife/do/ ShowContent/inspiration_expert_advice/expert_columns/Paul_ Chous/vitamin-d-levels.html.

Coulston, Ann M. and Carol J. Boushey (eds.) *Nutrition in the Prevention and Treatment of Disease, Second Edition.* Burlington, Mass.: Elsevier Academic Press, 2008.

Cox, Ashley. "Acai Berries: Super Food or Hype?" Scientific Blogging, October 8, 2008. Available Online. URL: http://www.scientific blogging.com/variety_tap/acai_berries_super_food_or_hype.

Dentzer, Susan. "Online Focus: Dr. Godfrey Oakley," a News Hour with Jim Lehrer Transcript, PBS. Available Online. URL: http://www.pbs. org/newshour/bb/health/july-dec02/spinabifida_oakley.html.

"Disorders of Nutrition and Metabolism." Merck Manuals Online Medical Library. URL: http://www.merck.com/mmhe/sec12.html.

Dolinoy, Dana C., Weidman, Jennifer R., Waterland, Robert A., and Jirtle, Randy L., "Maternal Genistein Alters Coat Color and Protects A^{vy} Mouse Offspring from Obesity by Modifying the Fetal Epigenome," *Environmental Health Perspectives*, Volume 114, No. 4 (April 2006): pp. 567-572. Available Online. URL: http://www.ehponline.org/members/2006/8700/8700.html.

Duyff, Roberta Larson, MS, RD, FADA, CFCS. *American Dietetic Association Complete Food and Nutrition Guide, 3rd Edition.* Hoboken, NJ: John Wiley & Sons: 2006.

Eijkman, Christiaan, "Antineuritic Vitamin and Beriberi," Nobel Lecture, 1929, Nobel Prize.org. Available Online. URL: http://nobelprize.org/nobel_prizes/medicine/laureates/1929/eijkman-lecture.html.

"Food and Nutrition Misinformation," EatRight.Org, American Dietetic Association. Available Online. URL: http://www.eatright.org/cps/rde/xchg/ada/hs.xsl/advocacy_3311_ENU_HTML.htm.

Garland, Cedric F., Dr PH, FACE, Edward D. Gorham, MPH, PhD, Sharif B. Mohr, MPH, and Frank C. Garland, PhD. "Vitamin D for Cancer Prevention: Global Perspective," *Annals of Epidemiology*, Vol. 19, Issue 7 (July 2009): pp. 468-483. Available Online. URL: http://www.annalsofepidemiology.org/article/PIIS1047279709001057/fulltext.

Graff, Steve. "MEK4, Genistein, and Invasion of Human Prostate Cancer Cells," GEN (Genetic Engineering & Biotechnology News), July 28, 2009. Available Online. URL: http://www.genengnews.com/news/bnitem.aspx?name=59128856.

Greer, Frank, MD, FAAP. AAP Newsroom Press Release, "New Guidelines Double the Amount of Recommended Vitamin D," American Academy of Pediatrics, October 13, 2008. Available Online. URL: http://www.aap.org/pressroom/nce/nce08vitamind.htm.

Holick, Michael F., MD. "Resurrection of Vitamin D Deficiency and Rickets," *The Journal of Clinical Investigation*, Vol. 116, Issue 8, (August 1, 2006): pp.2062-2072. Available Online. URL: http://www.jci.org/articles/view/29449.

Khymenets, Olha, et al. "Mononuclear Cell Transcriptome Response after Sustained Virgin Olive Oil Consumption in Humans: An Exploratory Nutrigenomics Study," *OMICS: A Journal of Integrative Biology*, Vol. 13, No. 1 (2009): pp. 7-19. Available Online. URL: http://www.liebertonline.com/doi/pdfplus/10.1089/omi.2008.0079.

Kiple, Kenneth F. *A Movable Feast: Ten Millennia of Food Globalization.* New York: Cambridge University Press, 2007.

"Kwashiorkor," Medicine for Africa. Available Online. URL: http://www.medicinemd.com/Med_articles/Kwashiorkor_en.html.

Latham, Michael C. *Human Nutrition in the Developing World.* Rome: FAO: Food and Agricultural Organization of the United Nations, 1997. Available Online. URL: http://www.fao.org/docrep/w0073e/w0073e00.HTM.

Leonard, William R. "Nutrition and Human Evolution," 2002, reprinted at Sobieraj.org. Available Online. URL: http://people.bu.edu/sobieraj/nutrition/EvolutionNutrition.html.

"Malnutrition News." Doctors without Borders. Available Online. URL: http://doctorswithoutborders.org/news/issue.cfm?id=2396.

Mayo Clinic Staff. "Gastric Bypass Surgery: What Can You Expect?" Mayo Clinic. Available Online. URL: http://www.mayoclinic.com/health/gastric-bypass/HQ01465.

Mead, M. Nathaniel. "Nutrigenomics: The Genome—Food Interface," Environmental Health Perspectives, Vol. 115 (12) (December 2007): pp. 582-589. Available Online at PubMed Central. URL: http://www.pubmedcentral.nih.gov/articlerender.fcgi?artid=2137135.

"Metabolism." Bio-Medicine.org. Available Online. URL: http://www.bio-medicine.org/Biology-Definition/Metabolism/.

"Micronutrient Information Center." Linus Pauling Institute, Oregon State University. Available Online. URL: http://lpi.oregonstate.edu/infocenter/.

The Micronutrient Initiative and UNICEF. "Vitamin & Mineral Deficiency: A Global Damage Assessment Report," 2004. Available

Online. URL: http://www.wsahs.nsw.gov.au/folate/documents/ VMD_global_damage_assessment.pdf.

"Micronutrients in Health and Disease." Health Providers' Section, NutritionMD. Available Online. URL: http://www.nutritionmd.org/ health_care_providers/general_nutrition/micronutrients.html.

Mieszkowski, Katharine. "Why We Can't Eat Just One," Salon.com, June 18, 2009. Available Online. URL: http://www.salon.com/env/ feature/2009/06/18/overeating/index.html.

National Center for HIV/AIDS, Dermatology and STI (NCHADS) and Clinton Foundation HIV/AIDS Initiative—Cambodia. "Ready-to-Use Therapeutic Food (RUTF) as a Food Supplement for Treating Severe Acute Malnutrition (SAM) in Children in Cambodia," July 9, 2007. Available Online. URL: http://www.foodsecurity.gov.kh/docs/ docsMeetings/RUTF-Training%20Presentation-ENG.pdf.

Navarro, Gloria Elena. "Health and Nutrition Information: Fact or Fiction?" Dietician Central, May 9, 2006. Available Online. URL: http://www.dietitiancentral.com/articles/ nutrition_information_fact_fiction.cfm.

The NCMHD Center of Excellence for Nutritional Genomics. "Concepts in Nutrigenomics," University of California, Davis. Available Online. URL: http://nutrigenomics.ucdavis.edu/nutrigenomics/ index.cfm?objectid=35170271-65B3-C1E7-0328AC9106D4DAFC.

"New Research by D*Action Member Dr. Cedric Garland Suggests Role Low Levels of Vitamin D Play in Cancer Development." D*Action, Grassroots Health, May 25, 2009. Available Online. URL: http:// www.grassrootshealth.net/press.

"Obesity and Overweight." Global Strategy on Diet, Physical Activity, and Health, Publications, World Health Organization (WHO). Available Online. URL: http://www.who.int/dietphysicalactivity/ publications/facts/obesity/en/.

Olivier, Rachel. "Neutrophils: A Potent Source of Immune Enhancement," Original Internist, December, 2007, BNet Find Articles: Health Care Industry. Available Online. URL: http://findarticles. com/p/articles/mi_m0FDL/is_4_14/ai_n24940335/.

Oyelami, O.A. and T.A. Ogunlesi. "Kwashiorkor: Is It a Dying Disease?" *South African Medical Journal*, January, 2007, BNET Find Articles.com. Available Online. URL: http://findarticles.com/p/articles/mi_6869/is_1_97/ai_n28448824/.

Passwater, Richard A., PhD. "Nutrigenomics and Pharmogenomics: Hope for the Future: An Interview with Dr. James Kaput," *Whole Foods Magazine*, August, 2008. Available Online. URL: http://www.drpasswater.com/nutrition_library/Kaput.html.

Perricone, Nicholas MD, "Dr. Perricone's Top Ten Superfoods," Perricone Lifestyle. Available Online. URL: http://www.perriconemd.com/category/perricone+lifestyle/superfoods.do.

"The Pima Indians: Pathfinders for Health." NIDDK Web site. Available Online. URL: http://diabetes.niddk.nih.gov/DM/pubs/pima/index.htm.

Porter, Roy. *The Cambridge History of Medicine.* New York: Cambridge University Press, 2006.

Rabinowitz, Simon S., MD, PhD, Mario Gehri, MD, Ermindo R. Di Paolo, PhD, and Natalia M. Wetterer, MD. "Marasmus," eMedicine from Web MD, May 20, 2009. Available Online. URL: http://emedicine.medscape.com/article/984496-overview.

Roizen, Michael F. MD, and Mehmet C. Oz, MD. *You: The Owner's Manual.* New York: HarperCollins, 2005.

Schwartz, Steven M., MD, FAAP, FACN, AGAF, and Michael Freemark, MD. "Obesity," eMedicine from Web MD, July 16, 2009. Available Online. URL: http://emedicine.medscape.com/article/985333-overview.

Shashidhar, Harohalli R. and Donna G. Grigsby, MD. "Malnutrition," eMedicine from Web MD, April 9, 2009. Availble Online. URL: http://emedicine.medscape.com/article/985140-overview.

Stice, Eric, PhD. "Healthy Weight Script," Healthy Weight Interventions, Oregon Research Institute, January 22, 2008. Available Online. URL: http://www.ori.org/Research/scientists/documents/HW_Script.pdf.

Sydenstricker, V.P., MD. "The History of Pellagra, Its Recognition as a Disorder of Nutrition and Its Conquest," *The American Journal of Clinical Nutrition*, 1958 Symposium Reprint. Available Online. URL: http://www.ajcn.org/cgi/reprint/6/4/409.pdf.

"Top Ten Humanitarian Crises of 2008." Medicins Sans Frontieres/Doctors without Borders. Available Online. URL: http://doctorswithoutborders.org/publications/topten/story.cfm?id=3236.

Tucker, Ross M., MD. "Iodine: Current, Historic, and International Perspectives: A Study in Persistence and Unanticipated Outcomes," Sarasota Memorial Hospital, May 1, 2009. Available Online. URL: http://www.smh.com/sections/services-procedures/medlib/education/podcasts/documents/tuckerMD_05-01-09-2.pdf.

UI Health Care News, "Advances Made in Fructose Intolerance Recognition and Research," News and Publications, University of Iowa Hospitals and Clinics, April 7, 2008. Available Online. URL: http://www.uihealthcare.com/news/news/2008/04/07fructose.html.

"The Universal Declaration of Human Rights." United Nations, December 10, 1948. Available Online. URL: http://www.un.org/en/documents/udhr/index.shtml.

"Updated Position Statement on Functional Foods Released by ADA," Medical News Today, April 3, 2009. Available Online. URL: http://www.medicalnewstoday.com/articles/144836.php.

Vitamin D Council. URL: http://www.vitamindcouncil.org/.

Watters, Ethan, "DNA is Not Destiny," *Discover*, November 22, 2006. Available Online. URL: http://discovermagazine.com/2006/nov/cover.

Weiner, Debra L., MD, PhD. "Pediatrics, Inborn Errors of Metabolism," March 30, 2009, eMedicine from Web MD. Available Online. URL: http://emedicine.medscape.com/article/804757-overview.

Williams, David B. "It's a Dirty Job, But Someone's Gotta Do It," *Earth Magazine*, August 28, 2008. Available Online. URL: http://www.earthmagazine.org/earth/article/68-7d8-8-1c.

Williams, Sue Rodwell, and Eleanor D. Schlenker. *Essentials of Nutrition and Diet Therapy.* St. Louis, Missouri: Mosby, Elsevier Health Sciences, 2003.

Young, Saundra, and Park Madison. "Group Challenges Acai Berry Weight-Loss Claims," CNN Health.com, March 23, 2009. Available Online. URL: http://www.cnn.com/2009/HEALTH/03/23/acai.berries.scam/index.html.

"Your Genomic Diet: Your Genetic Profile Could be the Key to Knowing What to Eat—and Staying Healthy," Article Excerpt, Technology Review (Cambridge, MA), Goliath: Business Knowledge on Demand, August 1, 2005. Available Online. URL: http://goliath.ecnext.com/coms2/gi_0199-4785690/Your-genomic-diet-your-genetic.html.

Zelman, Kathleen M., MPH. "10 Everyday Super Foods," Web MD, 2007 (Reviewed Dec. 4, 2008 by Louise Chang, MD), page 2. Available Online. URL: http://www.webmd.com/diet/guide/10-everyday-super-foods.

FURTHER RESOURCES

Abramovitz, Melissa. *Obesity (Diseases and Disorders)*. San Diego: Lucent, 2004.

Khumalo, Dr. Nonhlanhla. *Genes for Teens*. Cape Town, South Africa: Yigugu, 2008.

Miller, Jeanne. *Food Science (Cool Science)*. Minneapolis: Lerner, 2008.

Nardo, Don. *Malnutrition (Diseases and Disorders)*. Farmington Hills, M.I.: Lucent, 2007.

Schlosser, Eric and Charles Wilson. *Chew on This: Everything You Don't Want to Know about Fast Food*. New York: Houghton Mifflin, 2006.

Smith, Terry L. *Frequently Asked Questions about Celiac Disease*. New York: Rosen, 2006.

Sullivan, Robert. *Digestion and Nutrition (The Human Body: How It Works)*. New York: Chelsea House, 2009.

WEB SITES

American Institute of Preventive Medicine: "How Nutrition Works"

http://recipes.howstuffworks.com/how-nutrition-works.htm
A detailed article about the required macronutrients and micro-nutrients, when to use supplements, and fighting disease with nutrition and special diets

Body Mass Index: Centers for Disease Control and Prevention

http://www.cdc.gov/healthyweight/assessing/bmi/
Use the calculators to assess your BMI.

"Malnutrition in Ethiopia: Sheleme," Medicins Sans Frontieres five-part series
http://www.msf.org/search/index.cfm?searchCriteria=sheleme
Select the links for parts 1-4 and "Conclusion" for part 5. A series of articles about twin girls and their treatment for severe malnutrition by MSF doctors during July 2008.

MyPyramid.gov
http://www.mypyramid.gov/
Visitors can assess their current diets and develop a personalized eating plan for good health.

Phytochemicals: Dole 5 A Day
http://216.255.136.121/ReferenceCenter/NutritionCenter/Phytochemicals/P_Home.jsp?topmenu=1
Read about the health benefits of phytochemicals and use the interactive charts to find out about the phytochemicals in specific foods.

Scientific Facts on Diet and Nutrition: Prevention of Chronic Diseases
http://www.greenfacts.org/en/diet-nutrition/
A detailed summary of the WHO 2003 document concerning what is known and recommended about the prevention of disease with proper nutrition. It also includes a section about analyzing the reliability of scientific studies.

PICTURE CREDITS

INDEX

ABOUT THE AUTHOR

TONEY ALLMAN holds a BS in psychology from Ohio State University and an MA in clinical psychology from the University of Hawaii. She currently lives in rural Virginia, where she researches and writes books for students on a variety of topics. She has had an interest in nutrition and its relationship to health since reading Adele Davis's books as a young college student. Since that time, she is gratified to see that nutrition and disease prevention have now become mainstream topics of serious medial research.